The Web Empowerment Book

The Web Empowerment Book

An Introduction and Connection Guide
to the Internet and the World-Wide Web

*by Ralph Abraham, Frank Jas,
and Willard Russell*

University of California at Santa Cruz

SPRINGER-VERLAG TELOS THE ELECTRONIC LIBRARY OF SCIENCE

Ralph H. Abraham, Frank Jas, Willard Russell
Visual Math Institute, University of California
P.O. Box 7920, Santa Cruz, CA 95061, USA

Publisher: Allan M. Wylde
Publishing Associate: Kate McNally Young
Production and Manufacturing Manager: Jan V. Benes
Copy Editor: Paul Green
Electronic Production Adviser: Kimberly Michael
Cover Design: Ark Stein, The Visual Group
Cover Illustration: Stephanie Wooldridge

Library of Congress Cataloging-in-Publication Data.
Abraham, Ralph H., Frank Jas, and Willard Russell
The World Wide Web: An Introduction and Empowerment Book/
Ralph H. Abraham, Frank Jas, and Will Russell.

Includes bibliographical references and index.
ISBN 0-387-94431-1 (alk. paper)
1. Internet. 2. World Wide Web.

©1995 Springer-Verlag New York, Inc.
Published by TELOS ®The Electronic Library of Science, Santa Clara, California

TELOS is an imprint of Springer-Verlag New York, Inc.

9 8 7 6 5 4 3 2 1

ISBN 0-387-94431-1

THE ELECTRONIC LIBRARY OF SCIENCE

TELOS, The Electronic Library of Science, is an imprint of Springer-Verlag New York with publishing facilities in Santa Clara, California. Its publishing program encompasses the natural and physical sciences, computer science, economics, mathematics, and engineering. All TELOS publications have a computational orientation to them, as TELOS' primary publishing strategy is to wed the traditional print medium with the emerging new electronic media in order to provide the reader with a truly interactive multimedia information environment. To achieve this, every TELOS publication delivered on paper has an associated electronic component. This can take the form of book/diskette combinations, book/CD-ROM packages, books delivered via networks, electronic journals, newsletters, plus a multitude of other exciting possibilities. Since TELOS is not committed to any one technology, any delivery medium can be considered.

The range of TELOS publications extends from research level reference works through textbook materials for the higher education audience, practical handbooks for working professionals, as well as more broadly accessible science, computer science, and high technology trade publications. Many TELOS publications are interdisciplinary in nature, and most are targeted for the individual buyer, which dictates that TELOS publications be priced accordingly.

Of the numerous definitions of the Greek word "telos," the one most representative of our publishing philosophy is "to turn," or "turning point." We perceive the establishment of the TELOS publishing program to be a significant step towards attaining a new plateau of high quality information packaging and dissemination in the interactive learning environment of the future. TELOS welcomes you to join us in the exploration and development of this frontier as a reader and user, an author, editor, consultant, strategic partner, or in whatever other capacity might be appropriate.

TELOS, The Electronic Library of Science
Springer-Verlag Publishers
3600 Pruneridge Avenue, Suite 200
Santa Clara, CA 95051

THE ELECTRONIC LIBRARY OF SCIENCE

TELOS Diskettes

Unless otherwise designated, computer diskettes packaged with TELOS publications are 3.5" high-density DOS-formatted diskettes. They may be read by any IBM-compatible computer running DOS or Windows. They may also be read by computers running NEXTSTEP, by most UNIX machines, and by Macintosh computers using a file exchange utility.

In those cases where the diskettes require the availability of specific software programs in order to run them, or to take full advantage of their capabilities, then the specific requirements regarding these software packages will be indicated.

TELOS CD-ROM Discs

For buyers of TELOS publications containing CD-ROM discs, or in those cases where the product is a stand-alone CD-ROM, it is always indicated on which specific platform, or platforms in the case of a cross-platform CD-ROM disc, the disc is designed to run. For example, Macintosh only, Windows only, cross-platform, etc.

TELOSpub.com (Online)

Interact with TELOS online via the Internet by setting your World-Wide-Web browser to the URL: `http://www.telospub.com`.

The TELOS Web site features new product information and updates, and online catalog and ordering, information about TELOS, samples from our publication, data-files related to and enhancements for our products, and a broad selection of other unique features, Presented in hypertext format with rich graphics, it's your best way to discover what's new at TELOS.

TELOS also maintains these additional Internet resources:

`gopher://gopher.telospub.com`

`ftp://ftp.telospub.com`

For up-to-date information regarding TELOS online services, send the one-line e-mail message: `send info` to: `info@TELOSpub.com`.

Dedicated to

Pierre Teilhard de Chardin
1881–1955

Preface

After many years of daily UNIX and Internet activity, we came to be enthusiasts of the World-Wide Web while trying to choose an authoring system for a CD-ROM project. We decided to use Web software for the CD-ROM, thus seamlessly integrating the two disjoint worlds of CD-ROM publishing and the Internet. We are grateful to our publisher, Allan M. Wylde, for the initiative leading to that idea and then to this book.

As we enter the third millennium and complete the computer revolution, our future will depend on our creative actions taken today. The politics of cyberspace, our future world, are being determined *now* by those who are already empowered with full cyberfunctionality on the Internet – which today means the multimedia browsing capabilities of the WWW, the World-Wide Web. It is urgent that concerned people extend themselves as soon as possible into this new world, to participate in the creation of the future.

Our purpose in presenting this introduction and empowerment package is to enable as many people as possible to attain this level of citizenship in the future.

Turn on, boot up, and jack in! The future is ours to create.

Software Bundles

Here is a minimal suite of software for WWW connection, as described in the Bootstrap chapters in part 2 of this book.

Macintosh

Level 2:

- MacTCP^1, from Apple Dealers
- † InterSlip, from **InterCon** and free over the Internet.

  (800)223-9125, sales@intercon.com

Level 3:

- † Netscape Mosaic, a WWW browser from **Netscape Communications Corporation**. and free over the Internet.

  650 Castro St., Mountain View, CA

  (415) 254-1900, info@mcom.com

- † JPEG Viewer, from Aaron Giles, and free over the Internet

  182 E. 95th St. 11E, New York, NY 10128

  giles@med.cornell.edu

- QuickTime 2.0 and MoviePlayer, from Apple Dealers

---

1. † Each software package with this mark is available in our package on the Internet. Read the *bootstrap* chapters of part 2 for details.

Windows

Level 2:

- Chameleon, an Internet connectivity package from **NetManage Inc.**

  10725 N. DeAnza Blvd.

  Cupertino, CA 95014 1

  (408)973-7171, sales@netmanage.com
- Trumpet Winsock, shareware from Trumpet Software

Level 3:

- † Cello, a WWW browser from Cornell Law School's **Legal Information Institute**

  Cornell Law School, Myron Taylor Hall Ithaca, NY 14853

  lii@fatty.law.cornell.edu
- † WinGIF, an Image viewer from **SuperSet Software Corp.**

  PO Box 50476, Provo, UT 84605

- Player (an MPEG movie player) from **Xing Technology**,

  1540 West Branch St., Arroyo Grande, CA 93420

  (805) 473-7431

About the authors

Ralph Abraham is Professor of Mathematics at the University of California at Santa Cruz, Director of the Visual Math Institute, and is the author of a number of texts on mathematics, as well as *Chaos, Gaia, Eros* (Harper SF, 1994), and coauthor (with Terence McKenna and Rupert Sheldrake) of *Trialogues at the Edge of the West* (Bear, Santa Fe, 1992).

Frank Jas is a Lecturer for the University of California Extension Service in Silicon Valley, and **Will Russell** is Administrative Computing Coordinator at the University of California, Santa Cruz, UCSC. Working together as **J.R. International**, they have provided C and network training for engineers at companies from Amdahl to Sun. **J.R. International** also sells C source code for robust container classes and POSIX compliance packages (available on the Internet). Will and Frank got their start developing the first Internet-based enrollment system used by over 10,000 students each quarter to pre-enroll in classes and sections at UCSC. Database back-ends and NeXTSTEP GUI development projects are their current focus.

Acknowledgments

We are deeply grateful to John Abraham of Freestyle Studios, Ashwin Batish of the Batish Institute of Indian Music and the Arts, P.Q. and Sara Boomer from Boomeria Software Works, Evan Schaffer of Revolutionary Software, and Randy Kaemmerer of NASA, for extensive feedback on our manuscripts. Thanks also to Mary Eriksen for her work verifying the Internet provider data, Paul Green for his fantastic copy editing, and our publisher, Allan Wylde, for his patience.

Font Style Guide

Interactions between computer and human are generally shown in `Courier`, with the human responses you need to enter in **`Courier-Bold`**.

The names of UNIX utilities are shown in **`Courier-Bold`**; the names of Mac utilities are shown in **Helvetica-Bold**; the names of cross-platform and DOS utilities are shown in **Times-Bold**.

Menu entries are shown in ***Times-Bold-Italic***.

Host names, pathnames, URLs, and other specific values to be entered by a user should appear in `Courier`.

Most text is in Times Roman, the *default font*. New terms are in *italics* with definitions in the glossary. Words that should be *emphasized* when spoken are also in italics. Acronyms are in the default font unless they are also the name of a program (in which case they use the font for that particular utility).

Trademarks

This is an author-generated list of trademarks, their owners and originators, whose products and services are mentioned in this publication. Reference to them does not signify endorsement of the content of this publication by these trademark holders, unless otherwise indicated. The purpose of this listing is simply to inform the reader as to the rightful owner of these trademarks.

Trademark	Owner
Air Series	Spry, Inc.
Binhex	Mainstay, Yves Lempereur
Cello	Cornell University
Chameleon	NetManage, Inc.
CompuServe	CompuServe, Inc.
EINet	Engineering International
Fetch	Trustees of Dartmouth College
GN	John Franks
Hypercard	Claris Corp.
ImageViewer	Spry, Inc.
InterSLIP	InterCon Systems, Inc.
Internet in a Box	Spry, Inc.
JPEGView	Cornell University, Aaron Giles
Kermit	Columbia University
MPEG Player	Microsoft Corp.

Trademark	Owner
MacTCP	Apple Computer Corp.
MacWEB	Engineering International
Macintosh	Apple Computer Corp.
MediaPlayer	Microsoft Corp.
Mosaic	NCSA
MoviePlayer	Apple Computer Corp.
Netscape	Mosaic Communications Corp.
NetWare	Novell, Inc.
Netcom	Online Communications Services, Inc.
NextStep	NeXT, Inc.
Notepad	Microsoft Corp.
PKZIP	PKWARE, Inc.
Pentium	Intel Corp.
Player	Xing Technology, Inc.
Postscript	Adobe, Inc.
Procomm	Professional Communications, Inc.
Quadra	Apple Computer Corp.
QuickTime	Apple Computer Corp.
Samba	CERN
SoundPlayer	Microsoft Corp.
Sparkle	Maynard Handley
Stuffit	Aladdin Systems
TCP/Connect	Intercon Systems, Inc.
Trumpet-WinSock	Trumpet Software, Peter Tattam
Video for Windows	Microsoft Corp.
Win32s	Microsoft Corp.
WinGIF	SuperSet Software Corp.
WinWEB	Engineering International
Windows	Microsoft Corp.

Permissions

The System Folder Icon, Extensions Folder Icon, Mac Classic Icon, QuickTime Extension Icon and MacTCP Icon are copyrighted by Apple Computer, Inc. and used with permission.

InterSLIP, the InterSLIP icons, logos and documentation are copyrighted products of InterCon Systems Corporation (all rights reserved).

Trumpet Winsock by Trumpet Software International PTY Ltd.

StuffIt Expander and StuffIt InstallerMaker icons are copyrighted by Aladdin Systems, Inc. and used with permission.

Gopher, Bind, Finger, FTP Server, Mail Utilities, Mailbox, World Envelope, and TCP Crane icons are copyrighted by NetManage, Inc. and used with permission.

Contents

List of Figures

The Web Empowerment Book

Part 1   An Introduction to the World-Wide Web

In these first five chapters, we introduce the basic concepts of the World-Wide Web (WWW) and the look and feel of this new world, which is now self-organizing within the matrix of the Internet.

Chapter 1   Introduction

Many of us have wished for a miracle, to save us from crises such as the population explosion and environmental degradation. And now, it appears, that we have, in the World-Wide Web (WWW), a basis for facilitating that miracle. In fact, the WWW seems like a miracle itself!

It it easy for enthusiasts such as ourselves to gush poetic praise for the WWW, and we have and will continue do so. Unfortunately, many people have been frustrated by the enormous obstacles (temporary no doubt) in accessing this world of the future. Hence, this little package: a book and a network-accessible bundle of software to help you get started. Our goal is to give you enough of a paper tour of the Internet and the World-Wide Web to show you that getting connected is worthwhile. Then we want to provide the baseline minimum of explanation, reference material, and utility software to allow the reader to connect to the WWW from a personal computer with modem.

1.1 The history of the Internet

Beginning with the interconnection of machines at four universities (including two branches of the University of California) in 1969 under the name Arpanet, the Internet has grown by leaps and bounds, and is now a network of networks of phenomenal proportions[1]. (See Fig. 1-4.) Critical milestones in the growth of the Internet include the advent of the TCP/IP protocol standards for data packet transmission, the incorporation of these protocols in the UNIX operating system, and the development of Ethernet technology. Today, the

---

1. See Carl-Mitchell, Smoot, and John S. Quarterman, The recent history of the Internet and the matrix, RS/Magazine, July, 1994, pp. 24-27.

emergence of the WWW is driving the explosion of the Internet. (For more history, see the references in the Bibliography.)

1.2 Two classes of people

There are currently more than 20 million people on the Internet, and the number is growing by 80% per year.[2] A large portion of this growth is attributed to the WWW. And yet, it remains very difficult for most people to attain full citizenship on the Internet. What is going on? Obviously there are two kinds of people, the Haves and the Havenots. The Haves are mostly people at universities, government research establishments, and large industries. Many of these are professionals involved in building the WWW, which is truly a hard-hat area at present. The Havenots are everyone else. The main obstacles for Havenots will be analysed in detail in this book, providing a doorway to Havehood.

1.3 Five steps in the evolution of the WWW

We personally experienced the creation of the WWW in five key steps.

1. The UNIX world in the 1970s. Through the good fortune of working at the University of California, which became a main participant in the UNIX enterprise in its earliest days, the 1970s, we were fortunate to be given the gift of UNIX many years ago. We soon learned to use UNIX utilities such as

- `mv`, `cp`, `rm`, to move, copy, and remove files,
- `cd`, to change directories,
- `vi`, to edit text files,
- `mail`, to send e-mail,
- to write programs in **C**, and
- to compile them with **cc** and **make** (or eventually, with **gcc** and **gmake**).

These utilities and others are described in part 3.

---

2. See Calcari, Susan, A snapshot of the Internet, *Internet World* 5:6 September, 1994, pp. 54-58. Also, Quarterman, John S., and Smoot Carl-Mitchell, How big is the Internet anyway, *Microtimes*, 129, Nov. 14, 1994, pp. 64-72.

2. The Internet in the 1980s. In the 1980s, when the University of California system joined the Internet, we learned to roam the world with native UNIX tools, such as

- `telnet`, or `rlogin`, to login to a remote machine, and

- `ftp`, to transfer files to and from remote machines.

(These are also described in part 3.) Our professional activities became globalized, and creative cooperation extended around the world electronically, primarily using `mail` and `ftp`.

3. Anonymous ftp in the late 1980s. Using the UNIX command **ftp** requires having an account (or at least the password of an account) on a remote machine, as well as one on your own local machine. Its use amounts essentially to logging in to both of these accounts, and then transferring a file with the **ftp** commands **get** and **put**. In the long run, this is a terrific inconvenience, as you must tell each coworker or correspondent the password to an account on your machine, in which you want them to be able to put or get files. In a natural evolution, people began to have special accounts for this purpose called *anonymous ftp* accounts, which required no password; this useful convention led to a catastrophic increase in Internet traffic. Anonymous **ftp** still requires users to know the **ftp** command language in order to see what files are available, to change directories, and to get or put the files of interest.

4. Gopher in 1990. Next, we discovered new tools on the Internet, such as **gopher** in 1990 and **wais** in 1991, which were turning up with increasing frequency. It appeared that the Internet was a chaos of unbridled creativity! Clever programmers, professional and amateur, were making all kinds of new tools and distributing them freely over the Internet via `ftp`. The **gopher** system replaces anonymous ftp as a means of getting files, with a simple menu selection interface. The **wais** system provides an index of files available in the **gopher** network. Again, a tremendous increase in Internet traffic resulted from this innovation.

5. The WWW in 1993. And suddenly, the WWW burst forth as a new world (within the Internet) of hypertext, hypermedia, and multimedia opportunity, with its first graphics browser, **Mosaic**. (See Fig. 1-3.) This improves on **gopher** by merging its menus into text (thus, hypertext).

1.4 Personal computing in the 1980s

During this period, many of us supplemented our workstations provided by the university at work with PCs and Macs at home. Learning the peculiarities of MS-DOS and the Macintosh Desktop was very frustrating! We became beginners again, as we struggled to connect our personal machines to the Internet with modems, and to master new software that imitated UNIX utilities over the phone lines.

1.5 The obstacles today

And yet, this electronic cornucopia was ours only by default, through membership in one of the privileged institutions, the University of California. When we tried to access the Internet from our PCs at home, there were many frustrating difficulties. And if we were travelling, there were additional problems. Internet providers, companies providing for a fee what came from the University for free, revealed only a few UNIX tools, keeping the others hidden. For a beginner, these obstacles, along with the arcane jargon of UNIX, are daunting. For future reference, these are the main obstacles:

- finding an Internet provider, or gateway
- connecting the modem
- configuring the communications software
- learning the operating system of the servers (UNIX)
- learning the protocols and geography of the Internet
- empowering Internet tools locally (via SLIP or PPP)
- obtaining a WWW Browser

Thanks to a profusion of recent books devoted to some of these obstacles, many people have found their way well up this ladder to network heaven. Many others are stuck on a lower rung because, as of today, most of our local (toll-free for dial-in) providers do not provide the SLIP/PPP service that is required for full functionality on the WWW.

1.6 Four levels of citizenship

It will simplify matters enormously to quantify the onramp of the Internet in four steps. (See Figures 1-1 to 1-4.)

1. *Have modem will travel. At this level are people with a PC, a modem, and an Internet provider. This may sound like CompuServe, but it is not. CompuServe provides an e-mail link to the Internet, but no file access to Internet servers.[3] They provide their own forums, but no access to Internet news. Real Internet providers offer level 1 access to the full functionality of the UNIX operating system, with **mail**, **ftp**, **gopher**, and so on, as programs run on their remote machine.*

2. *SLIP me up, Scotty. At this level, one has all of the above, plus SLIP or PPP. This software, running on the provider's host, permits the local use of programs that substitute for the klunkier UNIX utilities **mail**, **ftp**, **gopher**, **telnet**, **wais**, and so on. Currently, this is an elite frontier, and it is this frontier to which the flood of recent Internet access books is devoted. (Some are listed in the Bibliography.)*

3. *Jacked-in to the WWW. At this level, one has all of the above, plus a WWW Browser, and multimedia Displayers for bit mapped images, digital video, and digital audio. You can browse the full multimedia wealth of the Web, discovering and learning an essentially infinite database spanning the entire globe. One can view, but not provide.*

---

3. The number of online accounts in the USA by July 1994 was 5.5 million, as reported in the New York Times of July 12, 1994. The number of level 1 citizens of the Internet at the same time, worldwide, is given as 18 million in Carl-Mitchell, 1994.

Using the World-Wide Web
Level 3
(mid-1990s: using a Macintosh and NCSA Mosaic WWW browser)

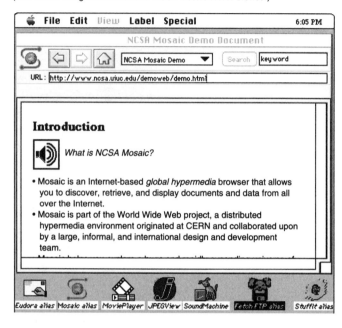

Level 3 of the network empowerment hierarchy.

4. *Totally WWWebbed. This level affords all the above, plus the ability to provide one's own hypertext, images, sounds, and videos. This represents full citizenship in the cybernautic universe.*

1.7 A miniature WWW FAQ

A curious and valuable feature of the Internet, common in Newsgroups, is the FAQ, a list of Frequently Asked Questions with answers. Here is a minimal FAQ for the WWW: the top seven questions.

1. *Why call it the World-Wide Web?*

Well, the Internet, as seen in Fig. 1-4, looks a bit like a world-wide web. We are not sure how this name got attached to the social organism called the WWW which is now self-organizing within the Internet. Perhaps it was just a synonym of "net" not yet claimed.

2. *What is the WWW?*

The WWW currently is estimated to comprise about 100,000 browsers and 5,000 server sites, with no comprehensive, up-to-date index. We may compare this to the telephone system of a medium-sized city in which you must call every store to inquire for help in locating another store, as there is no directory assistance! Eventually this may be rectified, but meanwhile the chaos can lead to some amazing discoveries. One can actually find almost everything within about a dozen jumps. Getting started is the hard part. After a month of browsing, what will you have found? A personal and totally unique universe of interactive information.

3. *What is unique to the WWW?*

Recently, **gopher** connected us to menus of plain text and multi media files, which we could transfer to our own computer. Now WWW browsers give us hypertext instead of menus, and automatically display the files in addition to transferring them to our machine.

4. *Who is on the WWW?*

The WWW sites include a large proportion of the governments, universities, science establishments, libraries, and large businesses of the world, as well as thousands of small businesses and individuals. Each site, of course, publishes only a limited amount of information. Larger institutions have larger hard disks to devote to publication on the WWW. Considering the federal fact books, tables of contents of magazines and journals at libraries, and so on, which are found on the WWW, you could regard it as the world's largest encyclopedia.[4] And it is undergoing continuous revision, which makes accurate indexing impossible. It cannot be trusted for accuracy in the same way as an authoritative printed book. Further, it has interactive environments as well as encyclopedic data, and has a life of its own.

---

4. In fact, the Encyclopedia Britannica is online, see the Webography at the end of the book.

5. *What is on the WWW?*

The World-Wide Web is a simple invention, and yet a gigantic innovation. It consists of three pieces which extend beyond the **ftp** and **gopher** of level 2:

- a new concept, the hypermedia browser,
- a new standard for hypertext files, HTML, and
- loose conventions for multimedia file types (image, sound, video).

6. *What is a browser?*

A browser displays hypertext files. The elevator bar (or scroll bar) represents the length of the entire file, so the height of the elevator itself is adjusted to indicate the portion of the file currently visible in a scrolling window. The first browser was created by Tim Berners-Lee at the European Center for Nuclear Research (CERN), in Geneva, in 1989. The first graphical browser was developed by Marc Andreeasen at the National Center for Supercomputing Applications (NCSA) during 1992 and released in January 1993. The browser he developed is called **Mosaic**. Besides displaying hypertext, it launches other programs to display image, sound, and movie files.

7. *What is hypertext?*

Hypertext is familiar to many PC users through Hypercard, and other similar programs. This is a text file with some words, symbols, or phrases identified by a change of font or color as hotlinks. After moving the mouse cursor to a hot link, a click of the mouse button initiates a jump of the mouse cursor to a different location in the file, or to a different file. The HTML format is a standard way of indicating hotlinks and their destinations, or anchors. Inline graphics are also supported: an image may appear on the page amid the text. These images may also be hot, that is, clicking them results in a jump to another file. It is this standard format for hypertext (HTML) that brings the second piece needed to build the World-Wide Web.

1.8 The plan of this book

Our specific objective is to boost people from level 2 to level 3 of this hierarchy. Necessarily, we must deal briefly with promotion to levels 1 and 2. The promotion process is divided here into three parts.

Part 1. This is an introduction to the concepts and reality of the WWW, and is best read in front of a browser connected to the WWW.

Part 2. The essential software for the empowerment process is bundled at WWW server sites maintained at `jri.ucsc.edu` and at `telospub.com`, for free and easy acquisition by anyone reading this book. The step-by-step procedure for this acquisition is given in part 2. One chapter in part 2 is devoted to Macintosh users, and two to Windows users. If you are eager to get connected and tackle the technical issues right away, then jump to those chapters.

Part 3. This is a crash course in UNIX literacy for beginners. You may need some of this material (especially the description of the **ftp** program) to obtain the software described in part 2, and then never have to use it again. On the other hand, achieving this literacy is very empowering in itself.

Start anywhere. The order of these three parts is arbitrary.

- You may need the *connection* of part 2 to follow the *introduction* of part 1, but you need the introduction of part 1 to achieve the connection of part 2.
- You may need the *literacy* of part 3 to complete the *connection* of part 2. But you may need the connection of part 2 to achieve the literacy of part 3.

We put these three parts in order of general interest: the most nerdy information is last. But after connection is achieved, you are always just two clicks away from the WWW!

1.9 Our mission

If it takes an entire book to describe how to get connected, is it worth it? Why struggle with these obstacles? Our conviction is that the WWW is one of the most important developments in centuries, if not millennia. If it is allowed to develop into its full potential without being crippled by legislation or over-commercialization, it may enable a major social transformation, and the creation of a sane future for humankind, in harmony with our environment. This possibility was described in detail by the French mystic, Father Pierre Teilhard de Chardin (1881–1955) in a series of papers, beginning in 1924. He envisioned the creation of a noosphere, enveloping the geosphere and biosphere, in a process of noogenesis much like the phase transitions of a neural net. This process, seen by him as beginning in this century, would culminate after about 500 years in a terminal evolutionary event, the Omega Point. The neural-net-like mechanism described by Teilhard de Chardin was one in which he predicted the gradual increase of the number and strength of links between individual human minds, which he called atoms.

> The actual number of atoms contained in complex units is of minor importance compared with the number and quality of the links established between the atoms.[5]

And that is exactly the promise of the WWW!

The 1990s have brought a new level of cynicism to the political scene in the United States. Some would argue that the word democracy hardly applies to a system in which less than 30 percent of the eligible voters choose to participate. The WWW is already being used to improve the level of citizen involvement in government, even at its highest levels. This is just one way in which the WWW could be a miraculous positive influence on society.

On the other hand, a further devolution of the world problematique might be an alternative outcome of the WWW revolution. The dire predictions of many critics may develop soon. What makes the difference? The presence of people, plain folks, world citizens, soon, in abundance, could make all the difference. And this is why we have written this book. So, turn on, boot up, and jack in, to the WWW

---

5. For an excellent description of this theory, as well as this quote, see Devereaux, 1989, pp. 135–143; and Russell, 1983.

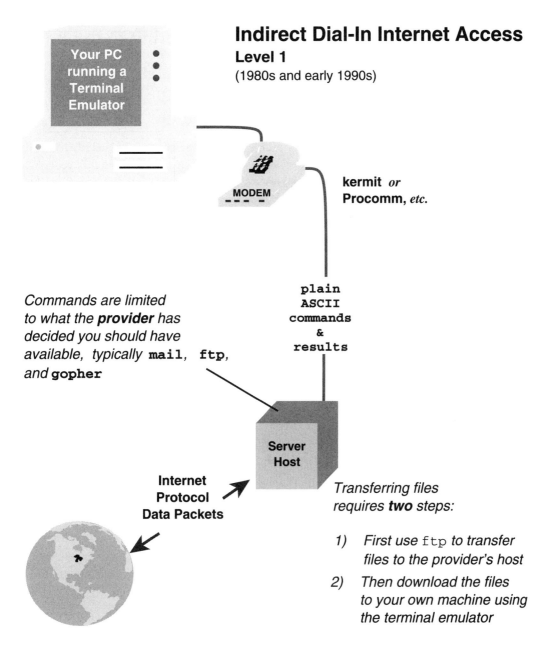

Indirect Dial-In Internet Access
Level 1
(1980s and early 1990s)

Your PC
running a
Terminal
Emulator

MODEM

kermit *or*
Procomm, *etc.*

**plain
ASCII
commands
&
results**

*Commands are limited
to what the **provider** has
decided you should have
available, typically* **mail**, **ftp**,
and **gopher**

Internet
Protocol
Data Packets

**Server
Host**

*Transferring files
requires* **two** *steps:*

1) *First use* ftp *to transfer
files to the provider's host*

2) *Then download the files
to your own machine using
the terminal emulator*

Figure 1-1. *Level 1 of the network empowerment hierarchy.*

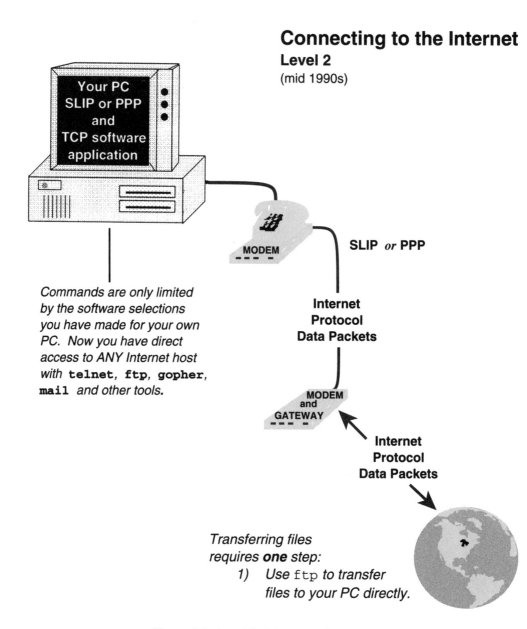

Connecting to the Internet
Level 2
(mid 1990s)

Your PC SLIP or PPP and TCP software application

MODEM

SLIP *or* **PPP**

Commands are only limited by the software selections you have made for your own PC. Now you have direct access to ANY Internet host with **telnet, ftp, gopher, mail** *and other tools.*

Internet Protocol Data Packets

MODEM and GATEWAY

Internet Protocol Data Packets

Transferring files requires **one** *step:*
    1) Use ftp *to transfer files to your PC directly.*

Figure 1-2. *Level 2 of the network empowerment hierarchy.*

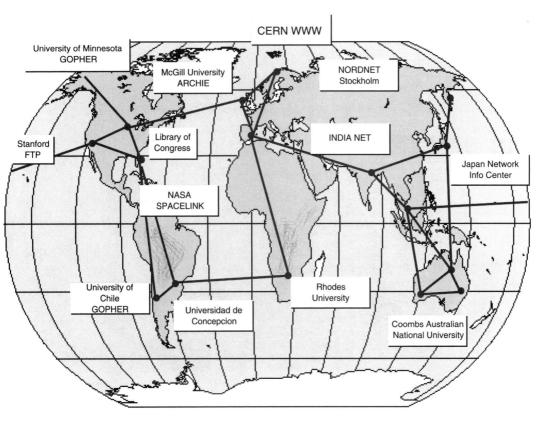

Figure 1-3. *Partial map of the World-Wide Web.*

Figure 1-4. *The home page for the U.S. President's residence.*

Chapter 2   **A Brief Tour**

2.1 The population of India

One day recently, during a public WWW demonstration, we were challenged by a question from the audience: What is the population of India? Never having looked for this kind of information before, we took a pretty inefficient route. But in about five minutes, we had the answer. Below is the list of jumps we recorded. Each of these jumps represents a mouse click on some highlighted text we read as we were browsing.

Figure 2-1. *We started this search with our friendly Mac Quadra 605.*

2.1.1 Home pages

Most server sites on the WWW have a master list of menus, like a table of contents, called its *home page*. Here we find an introduction to the site, its statement of purpose, and its personality. And almost every home page has a section called *Related Sites*, giving connections to other sites considered important.

2.1.2 First jump

- We started with our own home page at the *Visual Math Institute*. Since we know our own home page quite well, we zoomed through the bulk of the text and landed on Related Sites.

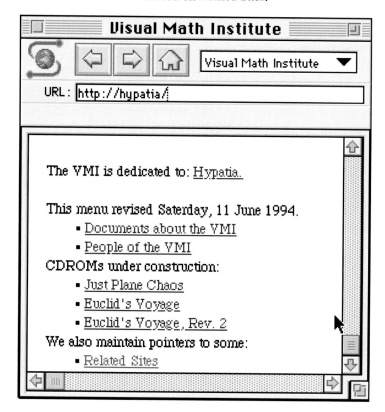

The window you see above is displayed by the program **Mosaic** (this is a Macintosh screenshot). Some things to notice from this window:

1. There is a *document title* listed in bold at the top of the window.

2. The spinning WWW icon, top left, appears to rotate when data is being transmitted over the network.

3. If you have to retrace your steps to get back to a more directed search, then you can use the left arrow at the top of the browser window.

4. The button with a little house icon inside takes you to your start page, which is the default page you have set using the preferences menu.

5. The small box showing Visual Math Institute and a down-arrow hides the history list. Press your mouse button here to see where you came from.

6. The scroll bar shows we are at the very bottom of the page.

7. The current URL (Universal Resource Locator, official WWW address) is shown in the little box labeled URL. This is the complete path of the currently visible document.

8. The resize button in the lower right-hand corner allows you to adjust the window to fit your screen.

A related site that seemed a good choice, based on experience, was EINet. They have a huge collection of topics arranged in a fairly easy-to-traverse set of pages. The EINet home page is a great jump station for just about anything you want to find, so we started there.

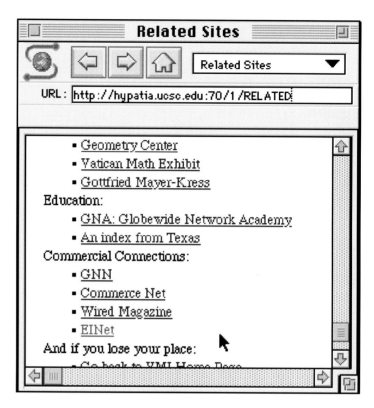

One trick to mastering the WWW is to find these great jump stations and keep track of them. That is what the hotlist mechanism is for.[1] Don't be afraid to use the hotlist mechanism for storing every page of interest. You can always go back to delete hotlist entries. It isn't as easy to remember them if they were never recorded in the first place. The wonderful thing about hypertext with WWW browsers is that they keep track of the long URLs. You just click on the highlighted text!

---

1. A hotlist menu item is available in most browsers. In this picture it is off-screen. It allows you to record the current URL path automatically, for later browsing.

If you follow a link you don't like, just use this left arrow to go back. ——

Further along in that same page

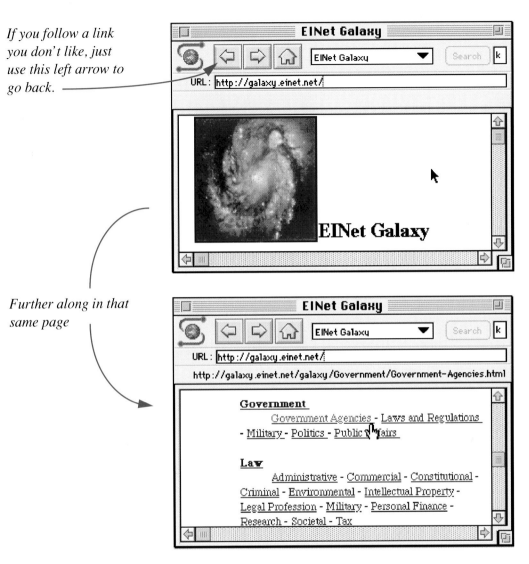

- In the EINet Galaxy home page are hundreds of highlighted links to other sites on a myriad of topics. We had to read through this list to find a link that would help us on our search for the population of India. We chose Government Agencies.

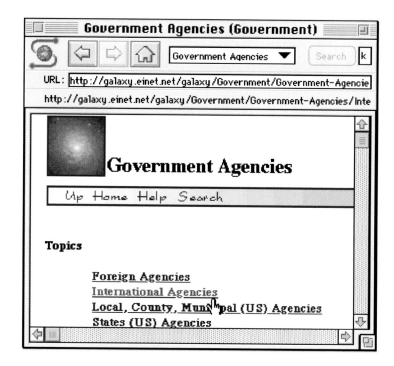

- On another page, government information was broken up into U.S. and International Agencies and we selected International. We could have taken a different route, but the wonderful thing about the Web is that all of the nodes are connected to all of the others in an infinitely diverse set of combinations and paths. If you try to reproduce our search, you may get to the same endpoint by having travelled an entirely different route.

Notice the box with the hand-written words Up Home Help Search in the Government Agencies page above. This is a *map*. Pushing on different regions (words in this case) would cause the browser to jump to another location. You can tell whether a graphic is *hot* (*i.e.* clickable) because it will have a colored border (typically blue). There are two *hot* graphics on the Government Agencies page, as well as some (underlined) hot text.

history list

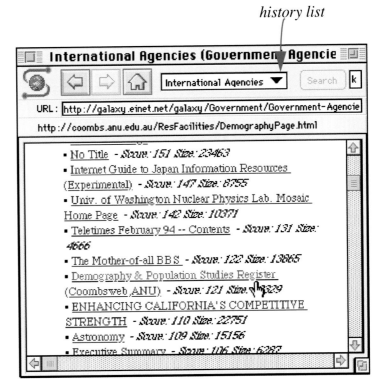

- In a long list of international agencies, the entry that promised to be closest to our goal was Demography & Population Studies Register (Coombsweb, Australian National University). Notice that we don't have to be intimidated by the fact that this place is in Australia. Our notion of space is transformed now from geographic space to hyperspace. The distance between any two points is not kilometers, but jumps. How many links do I have to follow to get somewhere? How much text do I have to wade through before I find an appropriate link or the information I want? How much time will I waste following inappropriate links? None of this time is really wasted, because you will be learning and storing hotlinks along the way for future reference. The next time you make this same trip through hyperspace, your journey will be aided by this experience! You will have earned a pith-helmet that you can proudly wear on future information safaris.

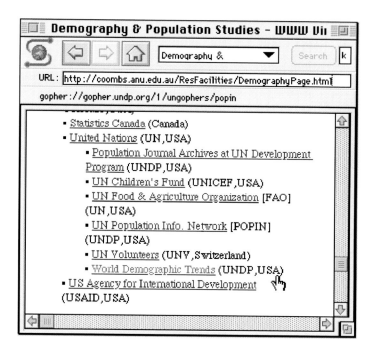

- Clicking to the Australian National University, we saw an entry for World Demographic Trends (United Nations Population Division).

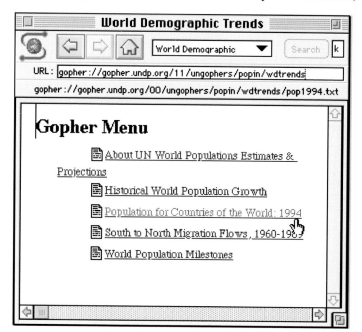

There were so many related pages that we had to traverse down into some of these links, and come back when we found that the information we wanted wasn't there.

Moving back along the route is easy. Using the WWW browser called **Mosaic**, there are two methods to backtrack. One of them involves the use of the left and right arrows, the other involves the *path list*.

Using the path list, you can see all of the places you have been since the last *branch* in your Internet search path. A path list is a pull-down menu with your current page showing at the top. A branch occurs when you traverse a link, decide it isn't the right one, back up, and then take a different route. The parent page is the point at which your search branched for a moment.

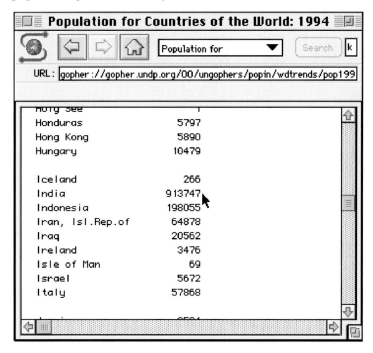

- Finally, we saw a listing for exactly what we had wanted – Population for Countries of the World: 1994

on which we found the answer – India: 913,747,000.

Warning: The WWW does not know everything. We were lucky with this search!

2.2 The secret is good guessing

Recently we wanted to find prices for computer printers from Hewlett Packard. We guessed they had a Web page and picked a name for their page which was most likely: www.hp.com. As you read through this book, try to identify the naming conventions for commercial, government, and educational information resources. As you acquire a mental list of favorite sites to visit it will become easier and easier to guess the locations of other resources.

2.3 Backtracking

During our hunt for population information we came across several pages from which we had to backtrack. One of them is shown below. They were intriguing, and they provided a lot of data, but not exactly what we were looking for. So, we retraced our steps and proceeded with the search you saw completed in this chapter. Some day we might come back to find out more about the World-Wide Web Virtual Library.

Here is one of the pages we stumbled on in our search for the population of India. This was almost our last jump.

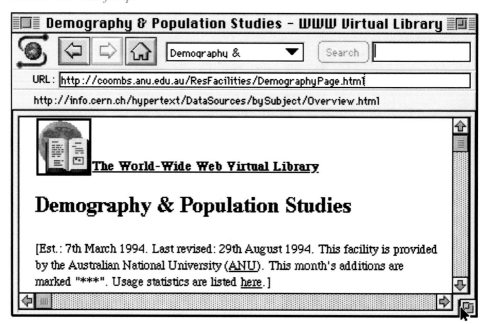

Figure 2-2. *World-Wide Web virtual Library.*

2.4 What is unique to the WWW?

In the 1980s, a program called **gopher** connected us to a world of plain text files. Now there are resources meant only for WWW, or hypergraphic browsers. For example:

- There is a private home site (aka *geek house*) in Carlsbad, California, which automatically takes a video shot of the beach every hour, digitizes it, and serves it on the WWW, as a visual surf report for the local surfer community.
- There is a third grade school room in the American Midwest which publishes art works done in class on the WWW.
- There is a collection of digital audio works by new and little-known composers and performance ensembles.
- Images of the comet striking the planet Jupiter were posted by astronomers as soon as they could be processed by the world's largest telescopes.
- Images inside a volcano taken by an eight-legged robot spider.[2]

Friends ask us:

- How can I use the WWW when I don't know what's out there?
- Do I have to know and type out all those long path names?
- Why does it all have to be so complicated?

The answers to these questions are what this book is all about.

Most of us use complex technology everyday. The difference between the easy-to-use technology (such as automobiles and televisions) and harder-to-use technology (such as VCRs and computer networks) is mostly determined by the amount of time a particular technology has been in use. Automobiles have evolved over a period of 100 years, VCRs over a period of 25 years, computer networks have only been on the scene in a big way for 10 years or so. The Internet and World-Wide Web are still close to, if not sitting on, the cutting edge.

---

2. See the Webography for URLs of the eight-legged NASA robot and others listed throughout the book.

2.5 How can I use it if I don't know what's there?

You have to hunt! A peculiarly British fetish is to plant a hedge in the form of a maze. For years people will enjoy the thrill of wandering through the maze to find out what surprise will be at the center. To explore the WWW, you just have to **pick a starting point**. It doesn't much matter where. Then, **jump!** Each bit of highlighted text is a silken thread that takes you to another part of the Web. When you explore a cave, you mark your trail with a thread that can help you find your way back. As if assisted by Ariadne herself, a similar trail is recorded for you in your *path list*. The path list is useful only in the current session. Extracting path names from your path list into your personal *hotlist* allows you to remember those pages in future sessions. The hotlist is analogous to your polaroid camera and journal from a real safari. To retell the stories of your Internet hunt, you click on entries from your hotlist and show people where you've been!

If you are not in the hunting mood, you can let a computer program hunt for you. *The robots are coming!* Robot WWW explorers constantly cruise the Web indexing new server sites. For example, the WebCruiser, the WWW Worm and the Mother-of-all-BBSs are listed in the Webography at the end of this book. E-mail word-of-mouth also brings in new and interesting sites daily. The WWW is growing too fast even for robots to keep up.

2.6 Chaos reigns in the Internet jungle

In the deep jungle the unwary explorer might have a feeling that all around was a tangle of uncontrolled chaos. Upon closer inspection and with more time, a subtle and unwavering order is discovered. The pathways through the Internet are similar. Our impression, after months of hunting, is that the Web is a scene of unprecedented creativity. There may be more individual and institutional creative energy in free play on the WWW than at any time since the Renaissance, and it has just begun. What appears to be happening (partly because of the total lack of inhibition by bosses and committees) is a major phase transition of the human intellectual sphere, an evolution away from the physically bounded communities of our animal ancestors to a conceptually bounded community that is totally human (in spite of its machine implementation). The idea of technology improving the interconnections of a global brain was predicted by Teilhard de Chardin in the 1920s. Now we are blessed with the reality of his prediction. You really must have a look! (See the Webography to get started.)

Figure 2-3. *A postscript tiger we bagged on one Internet hunt.*

Chapter 3   WWW Basics

Now let's review level 2 citizenship, being *connected* to the Internet, and then go on to level 3, being *jacked in* to the WWW.

3.1 The Internet at level 2

At this level we are able to connect from our own local computer to another person's remote machine over the Internet using a variety of tools. We presume now that this remote machine is a UNIX machine, like most *servers* on the Internet. The unfamiliar UNIX jargon we must use here will be explained soon, in part 3 of this book. But for now, you need to know that:

- UNIX is a multi-user operating system,
- users have private accounts and passwords, and
- user accounts have a home directory, as well as many other directories.

With a local machine connected to the Internet at level 2, and a user account on a remote machine also on the Internet, we may use the utility programs **telnet** or **rlogin** to connect, over the Internet, from our local machine to our remote account. This is similar to using the terminal emulators **kermit** or **procomm**, but the connection is more robust using TCP/IP[1] and the Internet. Our computer becomes a networked terminal accessing the remote machine so that we can issue commands there.

---

1. Transmission Control Protocol and Internet Protocol for sending data. These protocols are implemented in low-level software, to which we usually need not pay attention.

In addition to logging in to a remote machine, we usually have some files that we need to move over or back. The Internet provides a standard tool for transferring files called **ftp** (File Transfer Protocol), which has been around for more than 20 years. Unfortunately, in order to use **ftp** you have to be a known user with account privileges on the remote machine. In the past, this meant that someone had to create a separate user account for every friend with whom they wanted to share files. In the mid-1980s, people got tired of making these new user accounts, and the *anonymous* **ftp** system spontaneously developed. This is a convention under which machines have a fictitious user account, named anonymous, allowing direct access to a designated part of its filesystem from anyone on the Internet. This fictitious user requires no password, although it is conventional to enter your e-mail address in place of the password. The home directory of this account contains a folder, usually called ftp, pub, or public, with unrestricted access for reading, and sometimes writing. Whatever files are put there are regarded as *electronically published* material.

The files published for access via *anonymous* **ftp** could be of any type. Using *anonymous* **ftp**, servers around the world publish:

- text files (*.txt[2]),
- rich text (*.rtf),
- images (*.tiff, *.gif, *.jpeg, *.bmp, *.pict)
- program source codes (*.c, for example),
- binary files from thousand of applications,
- digital audio (*.snd, *.wav, *.ulaw),
- digital video (*.mpeg, *.avi, *.mov, *.vfw),

or any of thousands of other file formats in common use.

After obtaining the files on our own hard disk, we then have to quit the **ftp** program and launch some displayer of our own on the newly downloaded file. For example, under Windows we might use *Notepad* to inspect a text file. Hence, the Internet, for those on level 2, was developing as a multimedia encyclopedia of vast dimensions

---

2. By *.txt we mean anyname.txt, etc.

as long as ten years ago. Unfortunately, even after all that time it is still without a complete index!

It was the self-organization of the *anonymous* **ftp** system which led inevitably to the World-Wide Web, or level 3 of the Internet.

3.2 Enter hypertext: the WWW

The World-Wide Web is a simple invention, and yet a gigantic innovation.[3] It consists of three pieces which extend beyond the scope of level 2 (the anonymous **ftp** level):

1. standards for multimedia file types (image, sound, video),
2. *a new standard for hypertext files, and*
3. *a new concept, the browser.*

The first graphical browser was developed by Marc Andreeasen at the National Center for Supercomputing Applications (NCSA) during 1992 and released in January 1993. The browser he developed is called **Mosaic**. Rather than choose completely new formats for the kinds of files which **Mosaic** could handle, he decided to have **Mosaic** launch other helper programs to handle image, sound, and movie files. That way, **Mosaic** itself could stay small, while the other programs specialize in their particular formats. The file formats chosen will evolve over time, but the most common are:

- hypertext: `*.html`[4] (displayed by the browser)
- bit mapped images: `*.gif` or `*.jpg`[5] *(inline or launched)*
- digital audio: `*.snd` or `*.au` *(launched)*
- digital video: `*.mpg`[6] or `*.mov` *(launched)*

Hypertext is familiar to many PC users through HyperCard, and other similar programs. This is a text file with some words, symbols, or phrases identified by a change of font or color as *hot links*. After moving the mouse cursor to a hot link, a click of the mouse button initiates a jump of the mouse cursor to a different location in

---

3. The original idea and the first browser are due to Tim Berners-Lee at CERN in 1989.
4. Hyper Text Markup Language, HTML.
5. Joint Picture Experts Group, JPEG.
6. Motion Picture Experts Group, MPEG.

An Example of HyperText
(as displayed by NCSA Mosaic)

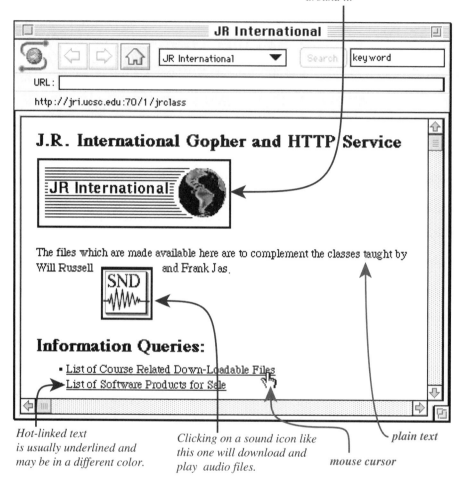

A hot graphic usually has a colored box around it.

Hot-linked text is usually underlined and may be in a different color.

Clicking on a sound icon like this one will download and play audio files.

plain text

mouse cursor

Figure 3-1. *HyperText displayed using Mosaic.*

the file, or to a different file. The HTML format is a standard way of indicating hot links and their destinations, or *anchors. Inline graphics* are also supported: An image may appear on the page amid the text. These images may also be hot; that is, clicking one results in a jump to another file. It is this standard format for hypertext (HTML) that provides the second piece needed to build the World-Wide Web.

The *browser* concept (the best-known of which is **Mosaic**[7]) displays hypertext or HTML files. The elevator bar (or scroll bar) represents the length of the entire file, so the height of the elevator itself is adjusted to indicate the portion of the file currently visible in a scrolling window.

3.3 WWW modes: http, gopher, ftp, wais, telnet

Mosaic and most subsequent browsers include the basic functionality of level 2: **telnet, ftp, gopher**, and **wais**,[8] as well as adding the ability to display hypertext using **http**.[9] In order to maintain backward compatibility with older servers, the browser must support a number of connection modes:

- *http mode*: affords level 3 multimedia access to the WWW,

- *ftp mode*: automates the **anonymous ftp** process, primarily for fetching a file which is not available on the WWW; easier to use than **ftp** under UNIX,

- *gopher mode*: searches **gopher** servers not yet upgraded to the WWW; navigates with key-stroke menus, just like **gopher** under UNIX, a menu interface for **anonymous ftp**,

- *wais mode*: used like **wais** under UNIX to access WAIS servers for searches, as with the " / " function in **gopher**,

- *telnet mode*: provides a terminal to a remote machine, like **telnet** under UNIX.

---

7. Many others exist, such as **Netscape** from Netscape Communications.
8. Wide Area Information Search, WAIS. This is an indexing system for the text of documents.
9. Hyper Text Transfer Protocol, HTTP, the heart of the WWW.

3.4 URLs: addresses on the WWW

Part of the WWW structure is a standard for specifying the location of a file on any machine anywhere in cyberspace. This world-wide pathname is called a Universal Resource Locator (URL). In order to provide access to any machine using any one of several connection schemes, part of the URL must specify the server's address in

Viewing Hypertext

The currently highlighted hot link is a "map." Clicking on a region within a "map" takes you to a different URL.

Elevator bar shows we are viewing a segment of text about 20% into the document.

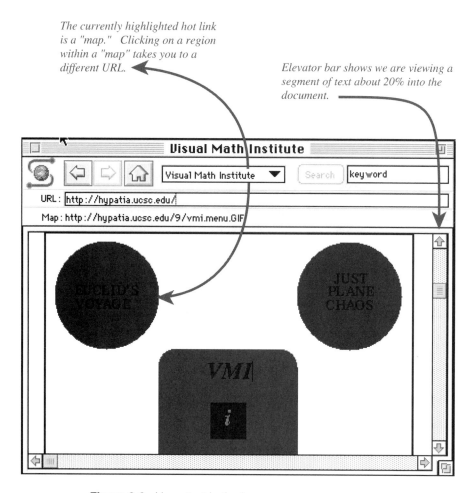

Figure 3-2. *Hypertext in the browser.*

cyberspace. This builds on the Internet addressing standard, which provides two equivalent addresses for each site:

- *IP address*, such as `129.32.300.12`, and
- *complete hostname*, such as `hypatia.ucsc.edu` (hostname `hypatia` and domain name `ucsc.edu`)

On the WWW, addresses are increased by an additional prefix specifying the connection mode. Hence:

- `http://hypatia.ucsc.edu`
- `gopher://hypatia.ucsc.edu`
- `ftp://hypatia.ucsc.edu`
- `wais://hypatia.ucsc.edu`
- `telnet://hypatia.ucsc.edu`

URL:
Universal Resource Locator

(specifies the path of a file anywhere in the world on any connected machine)

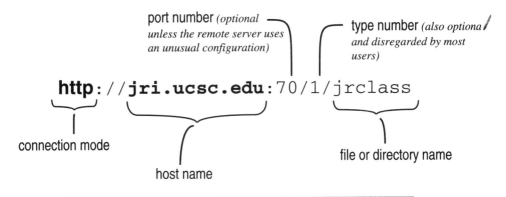

Figure 3-3. *URL structure.*

Note the colon and double slash. Also, there is a local mode:

- `file:/path/filename`

which accesses a file on your local machine as if it were served from a remote site. This is useful in previewing documents that you are creating to put on a server. You will be creating such documents when you get to level 4 of our empowerment hierarchy. Note the single slash in local pathnames, in contrast to the double slash for remote file names, which is required by some browsers.

A server can provide access to files using several connection modes. Our server supplies data to anyone using an **http** client (programs like **Mosaic** or **Cello**), a **gopher** client (the **gopher** program), or an **ftp** client (the **ftp** or **Fetch** programs). This way people who want to get our data can use the older software and still gain access. For a fancier view of these files, a WWW browser, which is capable of displaying HTML files using the **http** mode, gives you the most elegant format.

3.5 File types on the WWW

There are numerous file formats found on the WWW. Here are the standard types:

- **HTML** files, `*.html`

    This format is plain text, with inclusion of *tags* for simple style changes (bold, italic, fixed-width font, headers of six levels, etc.), *anchors* (either end of a hot link), inline images, and remote links to other documents. It is the basic type for WWW browsers.

- **GIF**[10] files, `*.GIF` or `*.gif`

    This is a bit mapped image format with lossless compression.

- **JPEG** files, `*.jpg`

    This is a bit mapped image format with lossy compression.

---

10. Graphics Interchange Format. Lossless compression means that after compression and decompression, the original image is regained, without loss.

- **MPEG** files, `* .mpg`

    This is the MPEG-1 standard for digital video, usually in a small format, with lossy compression.

- **SOUND** files, `* .snd.` or `* .au`

    These denote compressed formats for digital audio (there are many such formats, depending on the machine you are using.)

In addition, we frequently come across:

- **ASCII** files, `* .txt`

    This denotes just plain text, and

- **Postscript** files, `* .ps`

    Rich text and graphics, in a page description language suitable for sending to a Postscript printer.

3.6 Multimedia displayers

The display of an HTML file is one of the main jobs of the browser. The other file types are displayed by various *displayers*, or *helper applications*, and there are many choices for each type. In order to view inline graphics, the browser must have its own GIF and JPEG displayer, embedded within itself. For *side window* graphics a separate GIF/JPEG displayer is required. Likewise, for an SND or MPEG file, you need an external displayer for each. Thus, the minimum suite of software for multi-media WWW cruising is:

- HTML Browser (Mosaic, Cello, MacWEB, WinWEB)
- GIF/JPEG Viewer (JPEGView, WinGIF)
- SND Player (SoundMachine, MediaPlayer)
- MPEG Player (MoviePlayer, MediaPlayer)

3.7 The difference between HTML and http

The distinction between file types such as those listed above, and the connection modes is important. HTML is a file type. As we mentioned, this kind of file is a plain text file with tags (special formatting commands) mixed in. The method for transmitting HTML files efficiently over the network is called **http**. This is the low-level *protocol* by which hypertext is transferred. It is a low-level specification which insulates the users of an **http** browser from having to know some of the details of the links and graphics being displayed.

If you want to reach level 4 of our empowerment hierarchy – the level at which you run your own server – you will have to become familiar with HTML commands and the **http** server software. For now, at level 3, you need only enjoy the benefits of HTML and **http** as you cruise the information highway.

Macintosh Tools

Standard Internet Connectivity

Fetch FTP (File Transfer Program)
free from `ftp://ftp.dartmouth.edu/pub/mac`

Eudora (Electronic Mail Utility)
free from `gopher://gopher.archive.merit.edu/mac/util/comm`

Telnet (Network-Based Terminal Connection)
free from `gopher://gopher.archive.merit.edu/mac/util/comm`

Optional Tools

Stuffit Expander (public domain file decompression tool)
free from `ftp://ftp.ncsa.uiuc.edu/mac/utilities`

Stuffit Deluxe (compress/decompress and translation tool)
approx. $100 from `Aladdin Systems`
`(408) 761-6200`
`aladdin@well.sf.ca.us`

Figure 3-4. *Macintosh tools for level 2.*

Chapter 4   Hypertext

The standard transmission protocol for the WWW is **http**, and the default mode of the WWW is hypertext mode, from which the multimedia modes grow upwards, as branches from a tree. Once access to the WWW with an HTML browser is established, it is easy to learn a great deal about hypertext, and the WWW, just by browsing.[1]

Note: For hypertext browsing, there is a UNIX utility called **lynx** which can be used at level 2. Lynx is similar to another level 2 program, **gopher**. We might call this *level 2.5*. If you have achieved level 2 and you have access to **lynx**, we recommend practicing with this tool before going on to level 3. It is a text-based browser, and can show you all of the hypertext, but none of the graphics, of the WWW.

In this chapter we assume you have achieved level 2.5 (**lynx**) or level 3, and that you have a WWW browser at hand. If not, you can jump to part 3 of this book to get connected, and then return to this point.

4.1 What is hypertext?

Hypertext is text with *hot words* or phrases. Moving the cursor to a hot word and clicking the mouse button triggers a *jump*. (Some require just one click, while others need two clicks in rapid succession.) Clicking causes the browser to jump to another point in the current hypertext file, or in another such file. A hot word hides a *link*, which contains the URL of the destination site or file. This is known to the browser because it was transferred as part of the **http**, but you do not need to pay attention to these details.

---

1. For example, try out the jump stations listed in the Webography at the end of this book.

4.2 Your first jump

After starting up a browser, your first step is to request connection to a server site. Most browsers present a *Start Page* on starting up, with a list of interesting sites to click.[2] A list of interesting links is known as a *jump station.*[3] Many links on a jump station jump to another jump station, and so on. After jumping from station to station for awhile, you eventually arrive at a hypertext document to read.

4.3 A file is one long page

In the case of a full browser like Mosaic, MacWeb, Netscape, or Cello, while you wait for the transfer of the entire document from the remote machine to your own hard disk, you will be presented with a little movie for your amusement. One example is the elevator car shrinking within the elevator bar on the side of the browser window. When the transfer is done, the elevator bar represents the entire document, while the reduced elevator represents the relative size of the visible window. The concept here is that a hypertext file is one long page, which you must scroll through to browse its entire length.

4.4 Hot text and jumps

Now that we are in front of a hypertext file at last, we immediately see its chief characteristic feature: hot words or phrases, distinguished by underlining and a change of color. What results when you click on them may be discovered by experiment. Mostly, the results are understandable (and reversible) so go ahead and click everything. Chances are, each click on hot text results in either:

- a *browse window jump* to another location in the same document, or another document, which replaces the original file in the browse window, or

- a *side-window jump* involving the launch of a displayer or *helper application*. The destination file is downloaded temporarily to your hard disk when you click on certain links. The temporary file must

---

2. Usually the start page is a local file but occasionally, it may be a home page (described shortly) on a remote machine.
3. A jump station is a carefully selected hotlist.

have a name indicating which displayer should be launched (e.g., **.GIF** or **.SND**). The browser retains your place in the original hypertext, while the *side window* is created by the helper application. The helper application can be used to view the image or movie, to save the temporary file in a permanent location, or to print or discard the file, all without disturbing your browser. Using **Mosaic**, you pick which helper applications are launched by the various file suffixes under the menu choices: **Options->Preferences->Helper Applications.**

4.5 HTML format and anchors

The file displayed by the browser has been written in HTML. Someone at the server site has spent hours formatting and adjusting the layout of text and graphics using the commands available in HTML. Your browser knows the file is in HTML because it has the filename suffix **.html**. You often see the name of the actual file displayed in a small box at the top or bottom of your browser window.

In HTML, which is part of the WWW definition, each phrase of hot text is accompanied by an invisible *anchor*. The anchor is what specifies what will happen when a reader clicks on the hot text. The anchor specifies the target location in the same file, or the URL of another document on the WWW. The target URL is visible in a display box in the browser window.

Some hypertext functions are unavailable with **gopher** or **lynx**; they are reasons for getting a better browser that provides full access to WWW rather than just the text access available at level 2. These level 3 abilities are *inline graphics, side-window jumps, hot lists*, and *forms*.

4.6 Inline graphics, cold

cold

In addition to text, hypertext files may contain graphics known as *inline graphics*, which decorate the electronic page, just as we have come to expect in printed books. We may call these *cold inline graphics*, as they are not active when clicked. In the HTML format, these graphics are identified by pointers to external files containing bit mapped images (typically **GIF**.)

4.7 Inline graphics, hot

hot

Some inline graphics, *hot inline graphics*, are clickable. These may be distinguished from cold graphics by some subtlety of the browser, such as an underline under the graphic, or a blue border box. The possible results of clicking a hot graphic are the same as those of clicking hot text: you have to click to find out.

4.8 Inline hypergraphics (maps, imagemaps)

Inline graphics may also be *hypergraphic*, which means they are hotter than hot graphics. They may be clicked in different regions, resulting in different jumps for each region. We call these *hypergraphics*, *imagemaps*, or *maps*.

4.9 Side-window jumps

The links which result in side-window actions are those involving target files of any format other than `*.html`. For example, a plain text file, `*.txt`, may be displayed in a side window by a text editor. Graphics, sound, or video files, identified by their suffices, will be displayed by an appropriate displayer. As part of the configuration and customization process, you may specify which helper application on your machine will be called by the browser to create the side window for particular file types. For each suffix you choose a file type, for each file type you choose an application (e.g. Word, JPEGView, SoundPlayer, etc.).

4.10 Hotlists and bookmarks

Frequently, while jumping around the WWW, you may see an interesting page to which you want to return later for a more leisurely browse. Most browsers have a trick for this, called a *hotlist* or *bookmark*. Clicking the menu item **Add to Hotlist** or **Add Bookmark** adds the current URL to a file somewhere on your hard disk, which you may later edit with your plain text editor. Upon selecting the menu item **View Bookmarks** you may return to the interesting file with a single (or perhaps double) click.

*I clicked on a "hot graphic" from a NASA Web page.
The result was a side-window jump: a detailed
version of the same graphic displayed in a side
window.*

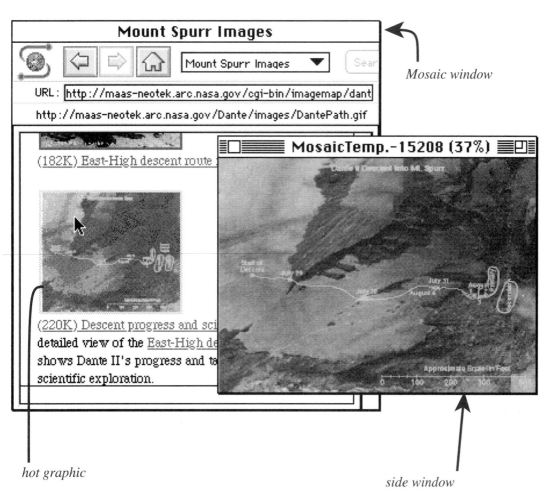

Mosaic window

hot graphic

side window

Figure 4-1. *Side-window jump.*

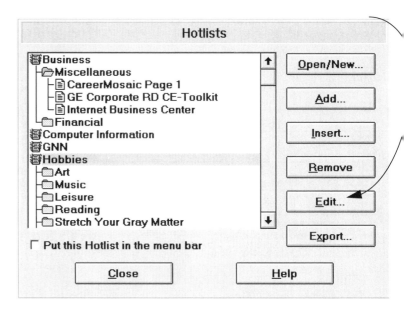

Figure 4-2. *The Windows Air Mosaic hotlist interface is nicely organized.*

4.11 Forms

Ordinarily, the communications you have with remote hosts are one-way. You click on a link and they send you more data. The idea of forms is to expand this notion allowing two-way communication. Not all browsers support forms, but those that do allow you not only to *receive* data that some Web site has published, but also allow you to respond to questions online, interactively. The server site can be set up to act on these responses in real time! We use forms to collect the names of people requesting information about our publications.

Other forms are used:

- to search a database,
- to vote in a poll,
- to have you enter mathematical or seed data and have the remote machine turn that data into an image, which is then displayed for you at your site, etc.

The Mosaic hotlist interface is a little awkward because you can open only one hotlist at a time. This version of Mosaic for the Macintosh doesn't remember from one session to another which file was the hotlist you were last using. You might have several hotlists covering different areas of interest which must be opened with this menu choice.

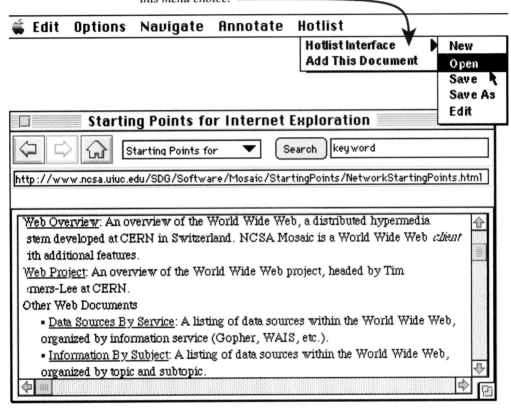

This "jump station" is offered by the University of Illinois. Most browsers have several "built-in" references to jump stations. This URL came up automatically when we pulled down the "navigate" menu.

Figure 4-3. *An early Macintosh Mosaic hotlist interface.*

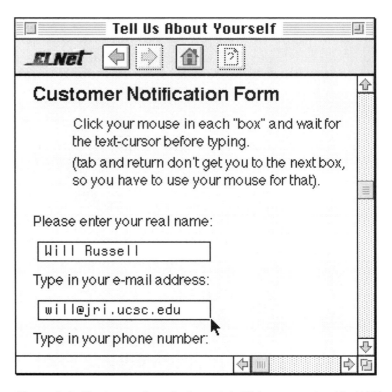

Figure 4-4. *The top portion of a form-style Web page, using MacWEB.*

Generally, forms have a button to push which causes the data you entered to be sent back to the remote server. The remote server uses the form data in different ways depending on how the Web page is set up. Earlier we mentioned that forms could be used to record information requests. The server could also automatically send e-mail or FAX you a document based on text you typed in the form.

The designer of a form-style Web page can use text boxes for recording arbitrary text, or check-off boxes which toggle an on-off value depending on whether you have clicked in them.

When all of the possible form boxes have been filled in, you push the *submit* button and the server goes to work processing the data you provided in an interactive session designed by a Web author perhaps half way around the world!

Some browsers don't show the submit button. In these browsers (such as Netscape Mosaic) hitting return in the last form entry has the same result as pushing the submit button.

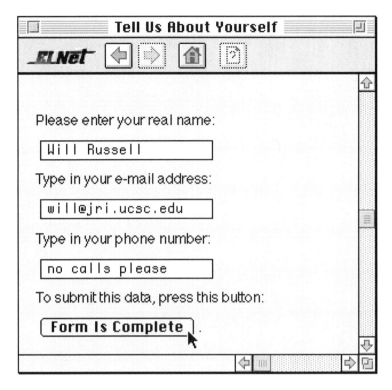

Figure 4-5. *The bottom portion of a form-style Web page.*

Chapter 5   Hypermedia

Hypermedia means multimedia in a hypertext context. This is part of the special appeal of the World-Wide Web, and also its main burden. There are two reasons why your access to World-Wide multimedia resources will be limited in the near future.

5.1 Traffic

There is a population explosion on the Internet, in which the WWW is a major factor, and we think that is just great! However, the expansion of the Internet capacity lags behind demand. The result is: *traffic congestion*. In terms of daily WWW life, this means that there are delays for connection to the more popular server sites, then there are delays for the *download*, the actual transfer of a file from the remote site to your own hard disk. Downloads of HTML files or TXT files are relatively quick, but other downloads (especially of multimedia files) may require an annoying wait of seconds or minutes, depending on the traffic congestion.

5.2 Speed limits

There is also the limitation of your own connection to the Internet. Whether due to your modem, your phone line, or the speed of your gateway, this bottle neck would limit your access to the WWW even if the Internet wires were lightning fast.

Due to these two facts of WWW life, you will not want to access every multimedia file available at sites you visit, even if they seem very appealing. This makes it important to understand the main file types found on the Web, and their typical sizes.

5.3 The future of the Internet

The major change in Internetworking over the next decade will be the speed at which data is transmitted. Even now, fiber optic cable is beginning to link major computing sites around the country, vastly improving the rate at which data can be provided. As cable-TV operators and telephone companies are deregulated, the mix of information available on this wiring infrastructure will change. New regions of the radio spectrum are being allocated for wireless modem communications that will dramatically change how people think of computing.

Another major change that will affect every facet of networking concerns the question of who pays for the infrastructure. For the past 20 years or so, the government has used tax dollars to install and maintain the information highway. Now the infrastructure has been privatized. In the coming decades, it remains to be seen whether the costs of network services will be shared by everyone and be available to everyone, or whether the networks will become an expensive resource available only to those who can afford it. Universal data access may one day be as crucial an issue as universal health care is in the 1990s.[1]

5.4 Graphics formats and displayers

While there are dozens of formats out there for graphics files, we will be concerned here primarily with one, the Graphics Information Format (GIF) adopted by the WWW. Sometimes these files are presented with a lower-case extension, `.gif`. This format, introduced in the 1980s by CompuServe, is used for *digital images* of different sizes and resolutions. The file contains a header, in which the essential format dimensions and the color code book are encoded. The image itself is compressed by a Lempel-Ziv algo-

---

1. Consult the EFF (see Webography) for updates on this.

rithm, a very efficient lossless compression method. Here are some parameters relating to the size of the compressed file:

- the pixel dimensions of the original image (e.g. 320 pixels wide by 240 pixels high, or 76,800 pixels)

- the depth of color information at each pixel (e.g. 8 bits, representing 256 colors or shades of gray, according to the color code contained in the header of the GIF file)

- the variance, or how much or little repetition occurs in the color data from pixel to pixel.

Such a bit mapped image as this page, for example, might occupy 100 to 200 kB (1 kB is 1024 bytes) in a GIF file. This could take several minutes to download, depending on the bandwidth of your connection.

Having obtained a GIF file in spite of these obstacles, how do you display it? Since the BMP format common to Windows and the PICT format native to the Macintosh are so different from GIF, a specialized viewer is required in either case. Some GIF viewers for each environment are freely available on the Internet. Part 2 of this book talks about the sources and instructions for getting this and other software by downloading from sites on the Internet.

For large images, it may be worthwhile to use a *lossy* compression algorithm to further reduce the size, instead of the *lossless* GIF method. In this case, the JPEG method (a discrete cosine transform algorithm) is emerging as a favorite. Thus, it is convenient to have a JPEG viewer available as well.

5.5 Sound formats and players

Formats for digital sound, as for digital images, vary from environment to environment. Sounds are conventionally sampled at 8, 22, 44.1, or 48 kHz, with 8, or 16 bits per sample, depending on the fidelity requirements.[2] These samples are then compressed by a variety of algorithms, usually lossy. The MPEG multiband algorithm is one of the most successful. Depending on the choice of all the

---

2. 44.1 kHz by 16 bits is Audio CD quality.

parameters inherent in the compression process, the size of a one-second digital sound file might be anywhere from 23 kB to 230 kB.

The format * . wav is native to Windows, while * . snd is native to the NextStep, * . au to the Sun, and * . aiff to the Macintosh and Silicon Graphics. The * . mpg format (part of the MPEG format for video plus sound) is very efficient, and is rising in popularity. Any of these sound file types may be encountered on the WWW, and there are various players available over the Internet.

5.6 Movie formats and players

Here also, we must acknowledge at least three different standards at present, the AVI of the Video-for-Windows environment, the MOV of the Macintosh QuickTime system, and the MPEG or MPG favored by the WWW. Fortunately there is a convergent evolution toward MPEG for all platforms. Three sizes are common at present: 704 by 486 pixels (full frame), 352 by 240 (most common now), and 160 by 120 (favored earlier). The latter smaller format is disappearing. The middle size can probably be viewed without any special hardware, using software packages that can decompress the movie files as you watch them at the normal rate. The larger movie with a 704 by 486 frame size requires (at the time of writing) a hardware accessory board to decompress and display at the intended speed of 30 frames per second.

MPEG display software for the middle size (352 by 240) without sound is freely available on the Internet. A short movie of just one second with no sound in this format will still need roughly 60 kB to 100 kB of disk space to store. Players for MPEG System files (picture and sound interleaved) are rare at present, and most MPEG movies found on the WWW will be silent.[3]

There are many variant formats of sound, images, and video.[4] If your browser fails to display a file, look at its filename extension. If the

3. The MPEG Player for Windows from Xing Technology is an exception, and is part of our recommended Windows bundle. Sparkle for the Macintosh also supports MPEG in software. Hardware MPEG decompression boards are currently selling at the rate of 100,000 per month!
4. For example, the GIF format is capable of storing animations. See *PC Magazine*, 13:19, Nov. 8, 1994, p. 336.

This is one frame of a short "movie" supplied by NASA showing the descent of their robot explorer "Dante" into the volcano at Mount Spurr. Movies are always displayed in side windows. This side window is displayed by the "MoviePlayer" application.

play

rewind and single-step

Figure 5-1. *One frame from a MoviePlayer side window.*

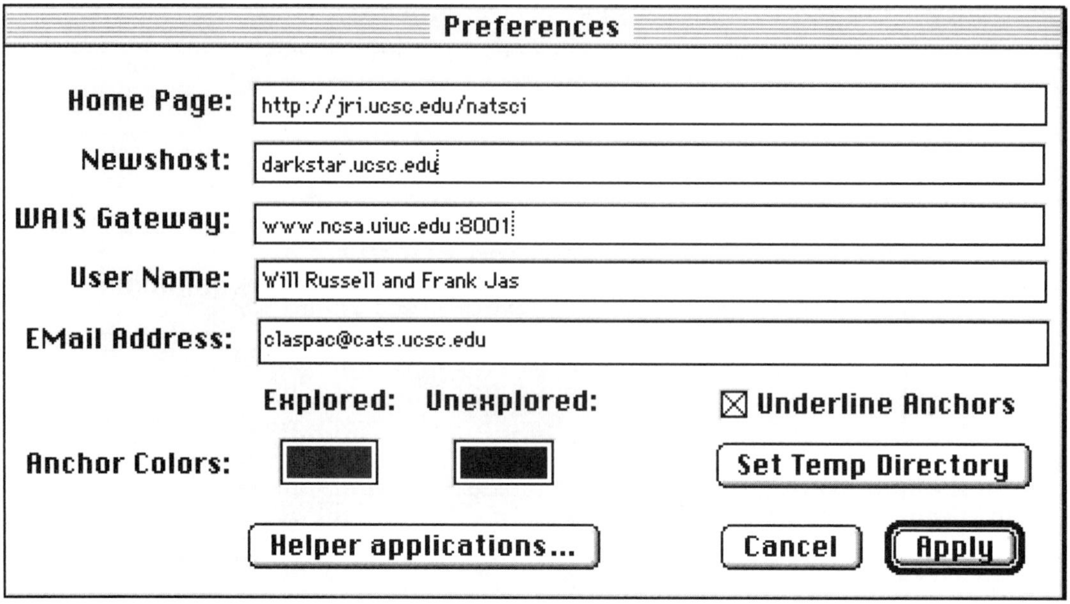

Figure 5-2. *Mosaic preferences dialog box.*

The Mosaic browser has a main menu called Options. *One of the entries there is* Preferences, *which brings up this dialog box.*

dot suffix of the file name is not listed in the **Helper Applications** for your browser, then you will have to find a viewer for that file type, install it on your system, and add the dot extension and application name to the list. However, we frequently encounter GIF files which the GIF viewer cannot open, and sound files which the soundplayer cannot play, and so on, due to differences in the way a particular software product generates these supposedly standardized formats. Standards are only effective if people adhere to them.

5.7 Other file types

Another type of file frequently encountered on the WWW, but possibly omitted from the list of helper applications, is Postscript, ***.ps**. This is an image description language developed by Adobe, Inc. It is powerful enough to be a complete programming language, and simple enough to be directly interpreted by most laser printers. A Postscript file can generally be sent directly to a laser printer to produce the pages of text as the author wanted. It is useful to have a Postscript previewer for your system to display the files on the screen before printing them.

The easiest format to download is plain text, ***.txt**. A common complaint of many Internet users is that some server sites put documents online in Postscript or HTML format rather than plain text. Postscript is fine if you want to print the text, but not if you'd like to extract sections of text into your own documents and databases for reuse and editing.

```
%!PS-Adobe- Adobe Systems 1986          0 0 moveto
%%DocumentFonts: Times Times-Bold        Bold setfont
%was Helvetica Helvetica-Bold            8 setflat % set flatness parameter
%%Title: letter_C.ps                     to 8
/Light /Times-Roman findfont 6           (C) true charpath  % obtain char
scalefont def                            outline
/Bold /Times-Bold findfont 200           clip  % use outline as the clip
scalefont def                            path
                                         0 144 moveto
/str (POSTSCRIPT-POSTSCRIPT-POST-        Light setfont % set the background
SCRIPT-POSTSCRIPT-POSTSCRIPT-POST-       font
SCRIPT-POSTSCRIPT) def                   26 {background} repeat
                                         % show /str thru the "C" clipping
/crlf{                                   path
         current point 6 sub             grestore
exch                                     showpage
         pop 0 exch moveto               %%Trailer
} def                                    % This program prints a fancy ver-
/background { str show crlf } def        sion
%%EndProlog                              % of the single letter C in the
200 350 translate                        % middle of a page.
gsave
```

Figure 5-3. *Example of PostScript program text.*

Document types are essential to the WWW. A formalism for classifying documents into types has yet to become completely standard, though an e-mail package called *mime* has provided the inspiration for the current classification. There may be several different file suffixes for one document (mime) type. For example, **.gif** and **.GIF** are both valid extensions for GIF files.[5] Each document type must have just one application which will be launched when files of that type are downloaded.

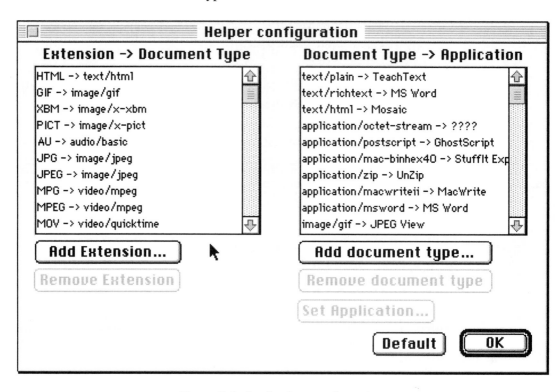

Figure 5-4. *Applications configuration.*

---

5. Guidelines may be found at:
http://www.ncsa.uiuc.edu/SDG/Software/Mosaic/Docs/extension-map.html

Part 2 Empowerment for the World-Wide Web

So you want to browse the Web! Someday, it will be easy to get started. But today, there is an obstacle course to negotiate. In this part, we guide you to your connection. You must:

1. Find a level 3 Internet access provider, that is, a SLIP or PPP provider. This is currently the most difficult step, but the situation is changing rapidly.

2. Obtain the level 3 connection software for your machine, so that it can speak SLIP or PPP. We provide this software (it is mostly but not completely free) over the Internet via anonymous `ftp`. If you have a level 2 connection to the Internet, you can download the software, following the instructions in this part, and in part 3. There are separate packages of software for the Macintosh and for Windows.

3. Install and configure the software for compatibility with your level 3 Internet access provider.

Chapter 6   Internet Access Providers

As we travel around proclaiming the magic of the WWW, we repeatedly come across a truly discouraging situation: There is actually no way to gain access to level 3 in many parts of the country.

6.1 The real obstacle

The problem is that many areas either don't have network providers, or, if the providers are available, they simply do not facilitate direct Internet traffic at level 2 or beyond. Those that do are called *Internet Access Providers*, or *IAP*s. In other words, you are limited to level 1 in most of the country. But this discouraging situation is changing rapidly. To locate an IAP near you, look in the Yellow Pages, or in *Internet World*.

To help you get started, we took the list (called PDIAL) of all providers known to the Internet itself, and called them up. We asked if they provide SLIP or PPP services. That is, do they handle direct dial-up connection to the Internet with TCP/IP[1] packet protocol? We recorded only the providers who claimed (as of August 1994) that they support either SLIP or PPP or both. We asked for the details, and entered them on this list.

By the time you read this, there will be many more providers than we have listed. For example, in our city, there are several new

---

1. TCP: Transmission Control Protocol; IP: Internet Protocol.
   We expect a new version of PDIAL while this book is in press. It can be found on the Internet at
   `ftp.netcom.com/pub/info-deli/public-access/pdial`.

SLIP/PPP providers in the past month alone. But, how to find them? They are not yet in the Yellow Pages. Nation-wide companies such as MCI will soon offer Internet services using standard modem technology, digital telephone technology (ISDN), and fiber-optics. Check with your telephone company to find out about their network services.

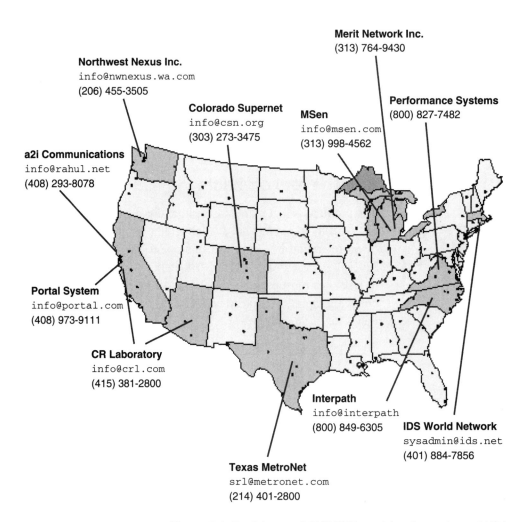

Merit Network Inc.
(313) 764-9430

Northwest Nexus Inc.
info@nwnexus.wa.com
(206) 455-3505

Performance Systems
(800) 827-7482

Colorado Supernet
info@csn.org
(303) 273-3475

MSen
info@msen.com
(313) 998-4562

a2i Communications
info@rahul.net
(408) 293-8078

Portal System
info@portal.com
(408) 973-9111

CR Laboratory
info@crl.com
(415) 381-2800

Interpath
info@interpath
(800) 849-6305

IDS World Network
sysadmin@ids.net
(401) 884-7856

Texas MetroNet
srl@metronet.com
(214) 401-2800

Figure 6-1. Partial map of SLIP/PPP providers in continental USA.

6.2 What is the difference between SLIP and PPP?

SLIP is an acronym for Serial Line Internet Protocol and it provides a mechanism for forwarding IP (Internet Protocol) packets over the serial port of your computer. SLIP does not provide a straightforward mechanism for initially establishing a dynamically assigned Internet address. (Believe us, this is a nuisance.) PPP is an acronym for Point-to-Point Protocol. PPP does everything that SLIP does, and in addition provides for the automatic configuration of dynamically assigned Internet addresses. Therefore, PPP is the better choice for most applications.

6.3 Alternatives to SLIP or PPP

Some providers don't offer SLIP or PPP services. In that event you may be able to get them to provide an alternative program which runs under UNIX on their machine, with a helper program on your local PC also. One example, called **tia**, is available from `ftp://marketplace.com/tia` for both Windows and the Macintosh.

6.4 List of Internet Access Providers by state

California:

a2i Communications

- dialup: (408) 293-9010 (v.32, v.32 bis) or (408) 293-9020 (PEP) 'guest'
- area codes: 408
- local access: CA: Campbell, Los Altos, Los Gatos, Mountain View, San Jose, Santa Clara, Saratoga, Sunnyvale
- long distance: provided by user
- services: shell (SunOS; UNIX; MSDOS) ftp, telnet, feeds, SLIP/PPP
- fees: sign up $15; 1 mth $25/mth,; 3 mths $16.50/mth; 6 mths $15/mth

- Mac scripts: SLIP/PPP dialing scripts provided by **a2i**
- e-mail: `info@rahul.net`
- voice: (408) 293-8078
- **ftp** for more info: `ftp.rahul.net:/pub/BLURB`

Portal System

- dialup: (408) 973-8091 high speed, (408) 725-0561 2400bps; 'info'
- area codes: 408, 415, PDN
- local access: CA: Cupertino, Mountain View, San Jose
- long distance: SprintNet: $2.50/hr off- peak, $7-$10/hr peak; Tymnet: $2.50/hr off-peak, $13 peak
- services: shell, ftp, telnet, feeds, IRC, UUCP, bbs, SLIP/PPP
- fees: sign up $19.95; $19.95/mth
- Mac scripts: No dialing scripts provided, write your own.
- e-mail: `cs@cup.portal.com`, `info@portal.com`
- voice: (408) 973-9111
- **ftp** for more info: n/a
- off-peak: 6pm – 7am plus weekends and holidays

CR Laboratory Dialup Internet Access

- dialup: (415) 389-UNIX
- area codes: 415,510,602,707,800
- local access, CA: San Francisco Bay area, San Rafael, Santa Rosa
  AZ: Phoenix, Scottsdale,Tempe, Glendale
  continental US /800
- long distance: 800 or provided by user
- services: shell, ftp, telnet, feeds, SLIP, WAIS
- fees: sign up $19.50; $17.50/mth
- Mac scripts: SLIP/PPP dialing scripts provided by **CRL**
- e-mail: `info@crl.com`
- voice: (415) 381-2800
- **ftp** for more info: n/a

Colorado:

Colorado Supernet, Inc.

- dialup: contact for number
- area codes: 303, 719, 800
- local access: CO: Alamosa, Boulder/Denver, Colorado Springs, Durango, Fort Collins, Frisco, Glenwood Springs/ Aspen, Grand Junction, Gunnison, Pueblo, Telluride; anywhere 800 service available
- long distance: provided by user or 800

- services: shell or menu, ftp, telnet, IRC, UUCP, SLIP, 56K, ISDN, T1, gopher, WAIS, domains, anonymous ftp, disk space, e-mail, to send text through a fax-modem
- fees: sign up $20 (Interactive Dynamic); connection costs: Mon-Fri: 8am – 8pm, $3/hr; 8pm – midnight, $2/hr; midnight – 8am, $1/ hr; Weekends: 8am – midnight, $2/hr; midnight – 8am, $1/hr; 800 number surcharge, $8/hr
- Mac scripts: N
- e-mail: info@csn.org
- voice: (303) 273-3475
- URL for more info:
  ftp://csn.org/CSN/reports/DialInfo.txt

Indiana:

IQuest Network Services

- dialup: contact for number
- area codes: 17, 219, 812
- local access: IN: Greater Indianapolis area
- long distance: provided by user
- services: BBS interface with e-mail, net-news, IRC, Telnet, FTP, Gopher, WWW, and Archie. Full SLIP/PPP at 14.4Kb, 28.8Kb, 56Kb or T1 speeds.

- fees: all prices are for 120 hrs/month: BBS @ 14.4Kb, $10/month; SLIP/PPP @ 14.4Kb, $15/month; BBS @ 28.8Kb, $15/month; SLIP/PPP @ 28.8Kb, $20/month.
- scripts: Fully preconfigured SLIP/PPP Software for Macintosh or Windows is given to you. The software includes some of the best graphical Internet software.
- e-mail: info@iquest.net
- voice: (317) 259-5050
- URL for more info:
  http://www.iquest.net/iq/iq_guide.html

Massachusetts:

Merit Network Inc. MichNet project

- dialup: contact for number or telnet hermes.merit.edu and type **help** at Which host? prompt
- area codes: 313, 517, 616, 906, PDN
- local access: Michigan; Boston, MA; Wash. DC

- long distance: Sprint, Autonet, Michigan Bell packet-switch network
- services: ftp, telnet, SLIP/PPP, irc, WAIS, gopher
- fees: sign up,$20; $20/mth
- Mac scripts: SLIP/PPP dialing scripts provided by **Merit**
- e-mail: sysadmin@ids.net
- voice: (313) 764-9430
- **ftp** for more info: nic.merit.edu

Michigan:

Merit Network Inc. MichNet project

- dialup: contact for number or telnet hermes.merit.edu and type **help** at Which host? prompt
- area codes: 313, 517, 616, 906, PDN
- local access: Michigan; Boston, MA; Wash. DC

- long distance: Sprint, Autonet, Michigan Bell packet-switch network
- services: ftp, telnet, SLIP/PPP, irc, WAIS, gopher
- fees: sign up, $20; $20/mth
- Mac scripts: SLIP/PPP dialing scripts provided by **Merit**
- e-mail: `sysadmin@ids.net`
- voice: (313) 764-9430
- **ftp** for more info: `nic.merit.edu`

MSen

- dialup: contact for number
- area codes: 313, 810, 517, 616; 800 service $5/hr in Michigan, $8/hr elsewhere
- local access: All of SE Michigan
- long distance: provided by user
- services: shell, WWW, Picospan bbs, ftp, telnet, SLIP/PPP, irc, WAIS, gopher
- fees: sign up,$20; $20/mth, $2/hr; with registered domain name and UUCP
- service: $35 startup and $35/mth
- Mac scripts: none provided, write your own
- e-mail: `info@msen.com`
- voice: (313) 998-4562
- fax: (313) 998-4563
- **ftp** for more info:
  `ftp.msen.com:/pub/vendor/msen`

New York:

Panix

- dialup: contact for number; also 800 access
- area codes: 212
- local access: New York, Long Island

- long distance: provided by user
- services: SLIP, PPP
- fees: sign up, $40; $35/mth
- Mac scripts: none provided, write your own
- e-mail: `info-person@panix.com`
- voice: (212) 741-4400
- **ftp** for more info: n/a

North Carolina:

Interpath

- dialup: contact for number; also 800 access
- area codes: 919, 704, 910
- local access: Raleigh, Chapel Hill, Charlotte, Durham, Fayetteville, Greensboro, Research Triangle Park
- long distance: provided by user
- services: SLIP, PPP, UUCP
- fees: sign up, $25; $35/mth (40 hrs), $2/hr thereafter
- Mac scripts: none provided, write your own
- e-mail: `info@interpath.net`
- voice: (800) 849-6305
- **ftp** for more info: n/a

Rhode Island:

The IDS World Network

- dialup: (401) 884-9002, (401) 785-1067
- area codes: 401
- local access: East Greenwich RI, northern RI
- long distance: provided by user
- services: ftp, telnet, SLIP, feeds bbs
- fees: sign up, $20; $20/mth

- Mac scripts: yes
- e-mail: `sysadmin@ids.net`
- voice: (401) 884-7856
- **ftp** for more info: `ids.net`

Texas

Texas MetroNet

- dialup: (214) 705-2902 9600 bps; (214) 705-2917 2400 bps
- area codes: 214
- local access: TX: Dallas
- long distance: provided by user
- services: shell, ftp, telnet, feeds, SLIP, PPP
- fees: sign up, $30; $16 – $19/mth
- Mac scripts: n/a
- e-mail: `srl@metronet.com`; `73157.1323@com-`
  `puserve.com`; `GEnie:S.LINEBARG`
- voice: (214) 401-2800

Virginia:

Performance Systems Int'l Inc.

- dialup: contact for number
- area codes: 202, 301
- local access: Reston VA
- long distance: provided by user
- services: SLIP, PPP
- fees: sign up, $200 1st three months includes complete TCP
  Intercom software; 4th month $29/29 hrs; $2/hr thereafter
- Mac scripts: yes
- e-mail:
- voice: (800) 82 PSI 82 or (800) 827-7482
- **ftp** for more info: n/a

Washington:

Northwest Nexus Inc.

- dialup: contact for number
- area codes: 206
- local access: WA: Seattle
- long distance: provided by user
- services: SLIP, PPP, UUCP feeds
- fees: sign up, $30; $30/mth (unlimited 2 hr sessions)
- Mac scripts: yes
- e-mail: info@nwnexus.wa.com
- voice: (206) 455-3505
- **ftp** for more info:
  nwnexus.wa.com:/NWNEXUS.info.txt

Chapter 7   How To Get Connected

We begin the connection saga with a review of the various levels of World-Wide Web citizenship. This time, we pay more attention to the network technology and software involved.

7.1 Level 1: No WWWay

Without a data connection to the outside world, a household is cut off from one of the fastest growing sources of information, opportunity, entertainment, and human-to-human interaction. This is the state of affairs in the majority of households. Critics of the Internet argue that only affluent households with money for computers, modems, and software will get to take advantage of the information super-highway. The same was true for the vehicular Interstate Highway also, and yet everyone in society helps pay for, and in some way benefits from, that system whether or not they drive a car.

7.2 Level 0: ASCII and you shall receive

The level 0 connection requires a PC (personal computer, Macintosh or MS-Windows, etc.) and a modem. Your modem and phone line connect you to a vendor-specific dial-in service, for which you pay a monthly fee. These services include CompuServe, America-Online, and so on.

In order to transfer data to your own PC when you are connected to the world at level 0 your provider would usually send you an easy-to-install custom terminal emulation package, on a disk specifically

Indirect Dial-In Internet Access
Level 1
(1980s and early 1990s)

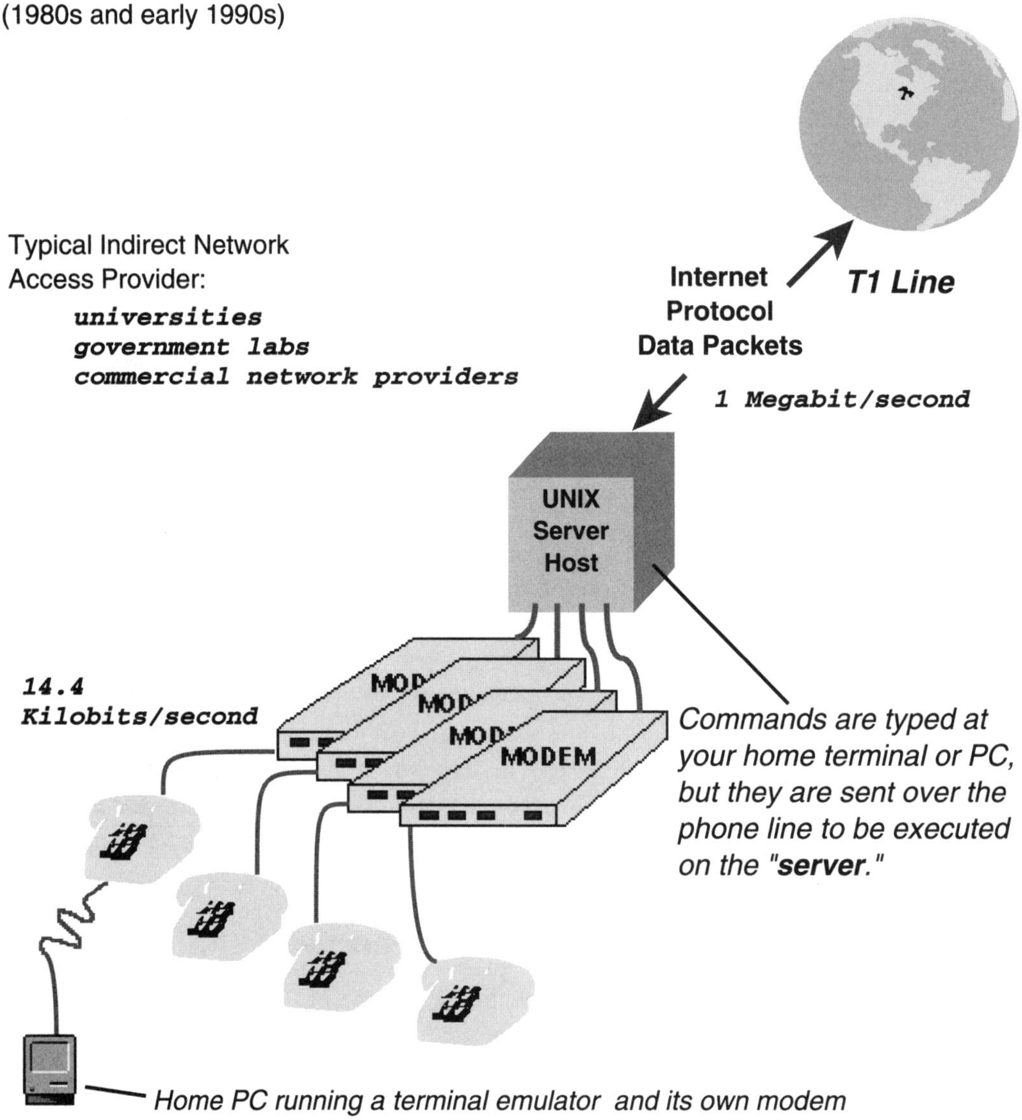

Typical Indirect Network
Access Provider:

universities
government labs
commercial network providers

Internet **T1 Line**
Protocol
Data Packets

1 Megabit/second

UNIX
Server
Host

14.4
Kilobits/second

MOD
MOD
MOD
MODEM

*Commands are typed at your home terminal or PC, but they are sent over the phone line to be executed on the "**server**."*

Home PC running a terminal emulator and its own modem

Figure 7-1. Level 1: Indirect dial-up Internet access.

meant for your kind of computer. These custom terminal emulation packages provide fairly simple menu options for downloading files. You can also upload files that you wish to share with others.

To transfer large amounts of data efficiently, the files are generally compressed and encoded into ASCII. When you are downloading a file using custom terminal emulation software, you may have options to decompress and decode the files automatically, OR you might be required to have other tools (such as BinHex or UnZip) to do this work by hand.

Unfortunately, these dial-in services have been set up to work only with the most popular hardware and software platforms. You can use America On Line or CompuServe easily from MS-Windows and the Macintosh. If you have an Amiga, UNIX, or other operating system, these services are horribly awkward, if not impossible.

At the time of writing, services such as America-Online and Compu-Serve do not provide Internet access; they provide their own vendor specific services. They do provide an electronic mail relay service which would let you send e-mail to Internet users *indirectly*, but this usually has an extra per-message fee. This situation may change soon, especially if you call up and request SLIP/PPP.

Learning to use the information services provided by one of these providers may be a lot easier than setting up a more direct Internet connection, but the skills you develop will be locked into that particular service provider, and limited to the topics and tasks that they decide are profitable for them.

7.3 Level 1: have modem will travel

Level 1 (indirect dial-in Internet access) providers in our area (Silicon Valley) right now are few in number. Most of these have a high-speed direct connection to the Internet that they use to connect their server to the world. Their server is typically a UNIX machine.

The UNIX computer acts as the server host and supports from 10 to 100 simultaneous users who call in on separate slower-speed telephone lines. The server has special hardware and software for accessing a high-speed Internet connection directly. It is the combination of a high-speed data link (using a special phone service called a T1 line) and the networking hardware/software provided with most UNIX machines that makes this computer uniquely suited to this task.

This level of connectivity will probably die out. The primary reason for the existence of this service has been the lack of satisfaction many people have experienced as they use the level 0 providers, and the lack of available software for home PCs to support a more direct connection to the Internet.

General purpose terminal emulators for accessing BBS services (which is what this style of access amounts to) have been around for 15 years or more. The most popular public domain terminal emulator is **kermit**. A terminal emulator comes with MS-Windows, or you can buy products such as **Procomm**.

7.4 Level 2: SLIP me up Scotty (Windows)

Direct **high-speed** TCP/IP Internet connections have been unavailable to most regular folks. Until recently, only universities, large computer companies, and some government agencies were willing to pay the expensive annual fees and the cost of the necessary wiring infrastructure. This kind of direct Internet connection allows an ordinary PC to be connected to the Internet at around 1.5 Megabits per second. Specialized TCP/IP packet software (SLIP or PPP) and hardware (an ethernet card) are added to the PC to make this possible. Software packages for providing slower **phone-based** Internet connections using a standard serial card (instead of an ethernet card) started becoming available in the early 1990s.

The collection of software which provides this TCP/IP connectivity is called in the jargon a TCP stack. This refers to the layering of software protocols required for network connectivity. An Intel machine running MS-Windows requires at least three layers of software. At the lowest layer is the packet driver, on top of that a library of I/O functions called WINSOCK.DLL; and at the top layer a TCP application such as **telnet**, **ftp**, **gopher**, or **mosaic**.

The WINSOCK.DLL provides a set of I/O functions which are supposed to be standard on any networked machine, regardless of

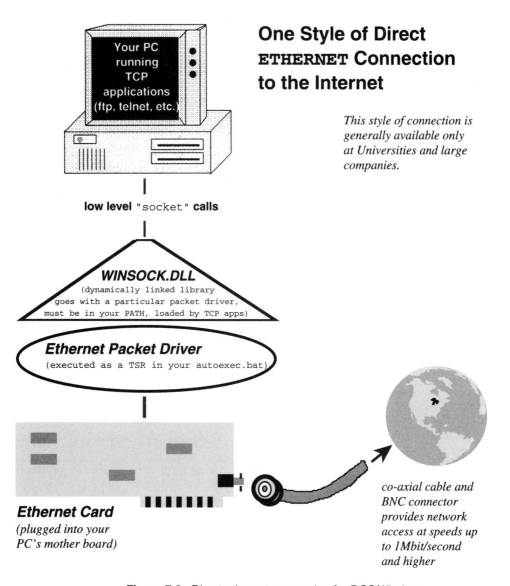

One Style of Direct ETHERNET Connection to the Internet

This style of connection is generally available only at Universities and large companies.

low level `"socket"` **calls**

WINSOCK.DLL
(dynamically linked library goes with a particular packet driver, must be in your PATH, loaded by TCP apps)

Ethernet Packet Driver
(executed as a TSR in your autoexec.bat)

Ethernet Card
(plugged into your PC's mother board)

co-axial cable and BNC connector provides network access at speeds up to 1Mbit/second and higher

Figure 7-2. *Direct ethernet connection for DOS/Windows.*

the kind of network connection. The WINSOCK.DLL is written on top of a hardware-specific packet driver and is usually supplied on the same disk as the packet driver. The disk is usually in the same box as an ethernet card or comes as part of a SLIP/PPP or serial-based TCP stack product (such as **Chameleon**). The packet driver is usually a TSR program (Terminate but Stay Resident in memory) that is executed in your autoexec.bat each time you boot the machine. The WINSOCK.DLL is not executed in the autoexec.bat, because it is dynamically loaded when the first TCP application needs those functions.

7.5 Level 2: SLIP me up Scotty (Macintosh)

Networking with the Macintosh is more convenient than with Windows. There are no explicit TCP stacks, no special plug-in cards to add, no IRQ levels to choose, and no IO ports to set. The Macintosh has a simple method for extending the features of the machine: You drop the icon for the added program onto the system folder and voila! In our case we dropped the **InterSLIP** control panel and the **MacTCP** control panel onto the system folder, rebooted, and we were connected!

7.6 Level 3: Jacked in and ready for action

It is easy to upgrade from level 2 (basic Internet connectivity) to level 3 (multimedia Web connection): All you have to do is copy a browser program such as **Mosaic** to your hard disk and launch it. The browser is good for displaying inline graphics and hypertext. To get the full capability for level 3, you must also have a set of side-window helper applications.

For the Macintosh, we use **JPEGView** for several different image formats, **SoundMachine** for audio clips, and **Sparkle** for MPEG silent movies.

The helper applications for Windows are **WinGIF** for displaying and converting several different image formats, and **MediaPlayer** (a standard Windows application) for playing audio clips (`*.wav`). **MediaPlayer** also handles MIDI files (`*.mid`) and video

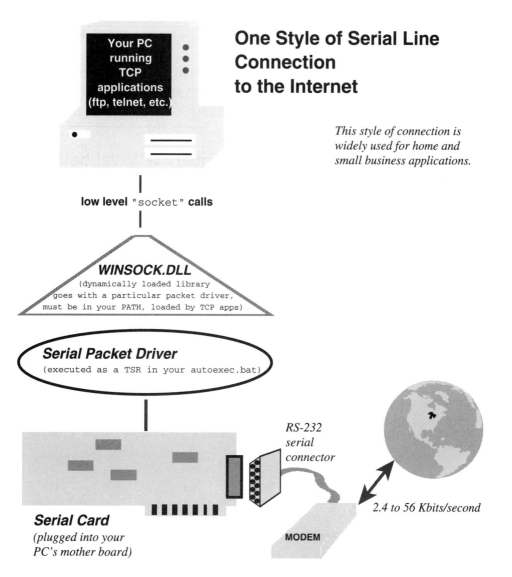

One Style of Serial Line Connection to the Internet

This style of connection is widely used for home and small business applications.

Figure 7-3. *Direct SLIP connection for DOS/Windows.*

(*.avi), but it assumes that you have added a sound or video card to your system and configured them correctly. Additional side-window helper applications for MPEG video, called **Xing Player**, and its partner for MPEG audio, **Xing Audio** are available from Xing Technology, and we have packaged these tools in our ftp-able WEB (Web Empowerment Bundle).

7.7 Level 4: Totally WWWebbed

 Full citizenship in the Web may be achieved with a Macintosh, a Windows PC, or a UNIX machine, running an HTTP daemon; or WWW server. Finding and installing this software is a job for real enthusiasts. After the software is installed, you have the fun of configuring your Web server and authoring your HTML pages. The server software we are using is called GN, and is available from:

```
ftp://ftp.nwu.edu
```

along with full instructions for its installation and use. The preparation of hypertext files in the HTML format is covered in WWW documents such as the HTML primer, found at:

```
http://www.ncsa.edu
```

Further help, if needed, may be found in more advanced WWW textbooks. For example, see Wiggins, 1994, in the Bibliography, or the WWW Tech jump stations in the Webography, at the end of this book.

Chapter 8   Macintosh Bootstrap

One of the reasons we put this book together was to make it as easy as possible to get connected. Part of that process involves collecting all of the software pieces. Since we have done this work for our own machines, we are in a position to share that work with you using the Internet itself to *bootstrap* you from level 1 to level 3. But first, here is what to do if you are already at level 2.

8.1 From level 2 to level 3

If you have (or have access to) a Macintosh already connected at level 2, you may use that machine to **Fetch** the software from the Internet onto a floppy disk. Then you can simply launch our custom installer package from the floppy disk. If you don't know someone who has such a machine, check with your network provider. If that doesn't work, take a couple of formatted floppies to your nearest college or university computer lab. Many libraries are starting to provide Internet access as well. Computer users groups and your local computer hardware dealer are also likely spots where you might be able to sit down at an Internet connected machine and use **Fetch** or `ftp` to transfer files directly onto the floppy disk you brought to take home for your machine.

8.2 From level 1 to level 3

Your first step before you can do anything with the Internet is to get an Internet access provider.[1] We assume now that you have suc-

---

1. See "Internet Access Providers" on page 59.

cessfully logged in to your provider's remote host at level 1 in our empowerment hierarchy. At level 1 you should be using a terminal emulator program to dial-in and indirectly access the Internet, using your home computer as a terminal for the provider's UNIX host. From that UNIX host you will be able to use *anonymous* **ftp**. The instructions are given in detail here and in Section 14.3 on page 153.

We have put together a package of the essential software (mostly public-domain) that you need to get from level 1 to level 2. This package is available from our server over the Internet. Here are the steps you will have to go through in order to get this package on your own machine

1. Login to your user account at your provider's server host using a terminal emulator.

We used **mac-kermit** to connect to our UNIX server at our campus.

2. Use **ftp** on the remote machine to transfer our package to your provider's host by making an **ftp** connection to our host jri.ucsc.edu.[2]

Here is a verbatim script of our session.

```
server% ftp jri.ucsc.edu
Connected to jri.ucsc.edu.
220 jri.ucsc.edu FTP server ready.
Name (jri.ucsc.edu:yourname): anonymous
331 Guest login ok, send ident as password.
Password:me@server.provider.net
230 Guest login ok, access restrictions apply.
ftp> ls -aCF
```

./	gn_docs@	menu
../	greeting.txt	natsci/
.cache	imagemap.conf	products/
arts/	images/	readme.ftp@
bin/	incoming/	sounds/
cgi-bin/	jr_mem.out	webstart.html

---

2. It is: /natsci/software/mac/network/tcp-slip-web.hqx

```
dwh/          jrclass/
etc/          map.default.html
ftp> cd natsci
250 CWD command successful.
ftp> cd software
250 CWD command successful.
ftp> cd mac
250 CWD command successful.
ftp> cd network
250 CWD command successful.

ftp> binary
200 Type set to I.

ftp> ls -aCF
./          ip_addresses.htmlnetnumbr.c
../          levels.rs          neturl.html
.cache      macextras.html     preview.ps
Address.ps mactcp.hqx          slip.hqx
ccl.txt     mactcp.html        t
dec.eps     macweb.hqx         tcp-slip-web.hqx
fetch.hqx   menu               via_ethernet.html
hypertext_desc.html            mosaic.hqx via_seial-
                               .html
interslip.html                 netlevels.html

ftp> get tcp-slip-web.hqx

150 Opening BINARY mode data connection
for tcp-slip-web.hqx (1214160 bytes).

1214160 bytes received in 5.91 seconds (2e+02
Kbytes/s)
Goodbye.
```

3. Use your terminal emulator to download the `tcp-slip-web.hqx` file to your own machine.

Since we used the program **mac-kermit** at home, we had to start up the remote **unix-kermit** server so that it could talk to our local **mac-kermit** about exchanging files. Again, here is our session script.

```
server-csh% kermit
C-Kermit, 4E(072) 24 Jan 89, 4.2 BSD
Type ? for help
C-Kermit> server

C-Kermit server starting. Return to your local
machine
```

4. We dropped back to our local **kermit** menus to use *Get File* for down-loading the `tcp-slip-web.hqx` file. We waited for a long time while the file was transferred (all 1.2 Mbytes).

5. You can use **binhex4** or **Stuffit Deluxe** to convert the `.hqx` file into a usable **Installer**.

6. Double click on the new **Installer** package to load all the software onto your machine.

7. Configure **MacTCP** with the **MacTCP Control Panel**. It should already be set to get its IP address from a *Server*; you need to fill in the *nameserver*'s address(es) and the domain name given you by your service provider (see more detailed explanation in the following pages, and Fig. 8-1).

8. Configure **InterSLIP** with the **Setup** application under the Apple menu. We have provided one sample connection entry. To start your own, choose *New* from the *File* menu (a more detailed explanation is in the following pages).

8.3 Configuring MacTCP and InterSLIP

MacTCP is a control panel application which extends the ability of your Macintosh so that TCP/IP-based applications such as **telnet**, **ftp**, **gopher**, and Mosaic can reach out to other machines on the network.

After you have installed **MacTCP** and the other software we have mentioned, you will need to configure your machine.

Most Internet Access Providers (IAPs) will assign Internet addresses to dial-up SLIP customers dynamically (at the moment you call). In order to make this work, you should configure

The MacTCP Control Panel

Depending on the hardware you have, you will see different icons to highlight. A single click configures MacTCP to use one of these different connection methods. After InterSLIP is installed correctly, its icon should be showing. Highlight that icon to use your <u>modem</u> for Internet access.

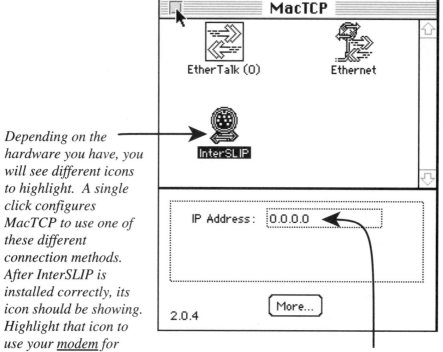

*The **IP** (Internet Protocol) address should start out this way because the actual address will not be assigned to you until your modem has dialed-up your network provider and requested a new Internet address. Push "More" to see and modify other details of your Internet connection.*

Figure 8-1. *MacTCP top-level control panel.*

MacTCP to get its address information from a server. That way, when you dial-in and first establish a connection using **InterSLIP**, the remote SLIP server will be able to assign you an address.

After Pushing "More" in the MacTCP Control Panel

*With the **Server** option set, MacTCP and InterSLIP will cooperate to set your machine's Internet address to a unique value each time you dial-in to your network provider.*

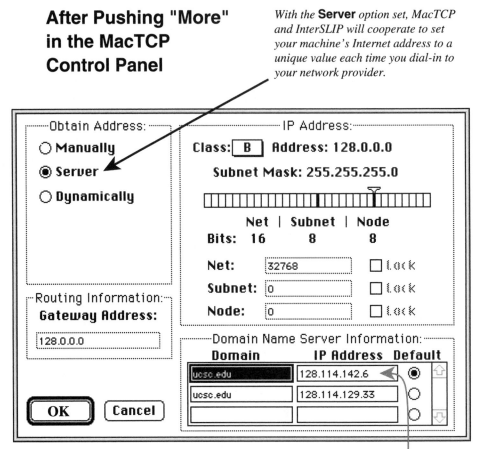

You will need to get the domain name and name-server address(es) from your Internet provider before you try to dial in. These fields must be modified with the correct information before any TCP application will work. Your network provider should be running a name-server that can tell your machine the IP addresses of any machine on the network.

Figure 8-2. *MacTCP detail control panel.*

Before you try to dial-in via modem, you will have to subscribe to an IAP. They should give you:

- modem telephone number (e.g., **408,425,1314**)
- name-server address (e.g., **128.114.142.6**)
- gateway address (e.g., **128.114.142.252**)
- the domain name (e.g., **ucsc.edu**)
- a connection script

To use the SLIP service from your own network provider, you will have to modify the phone number, name server, domain name, and connection script information in the **InterSLIP Setup** application.

8.4 Internet addresses

An Internet address is used to uniquely identify any one of the millions of machines currently attached to the Internet. Every one of these computers has to have a unique 32-bit number associated with it.

Your IAP will assign this number to you. To make it easy to write out 32 bits, each address is written as four 8-bit numbers.

At UCSC we have over 2000 computers connected to the network. In order to connect thousands of machines and give them all unique Internet numbers, we vary the last 16 bits of our Internet addresses. This last sixteen bits is broken into an 8-bit subnet number and an 8-bit host (or node) number. See Figure 8.3. The number **131** in the diagram designates the *subnet* to which a machine is connected. Within that subnet there are up to 255 computers that could be connected; the machine shown is *host* **153** in *subnet* **131** in the *domain* **128.114**. It is much easier for most people to remember a name such as jr660mac.ucsc.edu than these numbers.

Under all connection schemes (SLIP, PPP, or direct ethernet) you must know the names and IP addresses of your *name-server(s)*. If you use an ethernet card, you may also have to know the *network number* that has been assigned to each hard-wired computer. With **MacTCP** and **InterSLIP**, you should not have to hard code the network numbers or your own IP address. The *Server* option under **MacTCP** allows it to get the configuration from the provider's machine when you dial in.

8.5 What is a network gateway?

Your computer will be connected to the Internet on one of many thousands of small network segments. Each network segment can be thought of as a length of wire which may or may not have modems or some other hardware supporting it. These subnets are connected in turn to thousands of institutional network backbones, and the backbones are connected together between all of the regional and institutional networks througout the world. To join two or more network segments requires a specialized piece of hardware for forwarding the data packets from one segment (like the one you'll be on) to another. This hardware can come in many flavors, the most common of which is called a *gateway*. The address of the gateway machine on your subnet is a vital piece of information you may be required to get from your Internet provider. Some providers will have software to automatically tell your computer the gateway address. Other arrangements may work only if you fill in the configuration of the gateway address by hand.

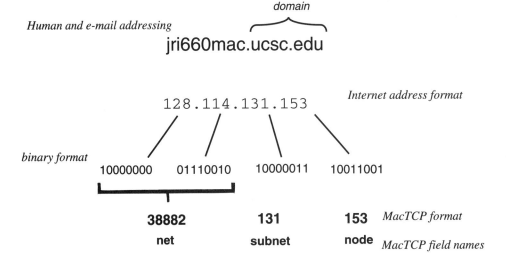

Figure 8-3. *Internet addresses in detail.*

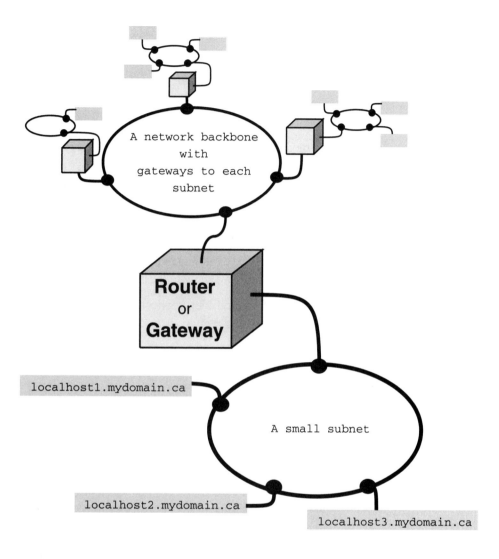

localhost1.mydomain.ca

localhost2.mydomain.ca

localhost3.mydomain.ca

A *gateway* copies packets from one network segment to another, but filters out those which aren't intended for the "other side."

A *repeater* and a *bridge* also copy data from one network segment to another. A repeater copies the data as signals (noise and all), while a bridge copies packets more cleanly, but neither do filtering.

A *router* is a smart gateway with more than two segments attached.

Figure 8-4. *The Internet is a network of networks connected by gateways.*

8.6 Activating an InterSLIP connection

At this point we will assume that you have managed to get our Installer package onto your own Macintosh. Now the fun begins.

Earlier we mentioned that you would need these pieces of information from your IAP:

- modem telephone number (e.g., **408,425,1314**)
- name server address (e.g., **128.114.142.6**)
- gateway address (e.g., **128.114.142.252**)
- domain name (e.g., **ucsc.edu**)
- a connection script

Now you will have to fill in these pieces of information in the configuration windows we show in the diagrams throughout this chapter.

Both **MacTCP** and each connection entry under **InterSLIP Setup** require the *nameserver*'s IP address to be filled in.

The **InterSLIP Setup** application will also need to know about your modem speed (*baud* rate), modem port, and most importantly it needs to know about a *dial script* and *connection script*.

8.6.1 Modem dial scripts

A dial script is a plain text file which describes the interaction that your modem is expecting when it is supposed to dial out. Many applications that use modems (FAX, terminal emulation, etc.) can use a similar dialing script, so don't try to start from scratch with this one. We have provided a dialing script for Hayes-compatible modems. Writing ***dialing scripts*** is a fine art and can't really be discussed in detail here. Fortunately, Hayes compatibility has become the de-facto industry standard and so the script we have supplied should work for 80 percent of the modems available.

The InterSLIP Setup application is typically placed in the Apple Menu Items folder so that you can easily activate your SLIP connection by pulling down the Apple Menu.

To create your own connection file, start up the InterSLIP Setup application and then choose "New" from the **File** menu.

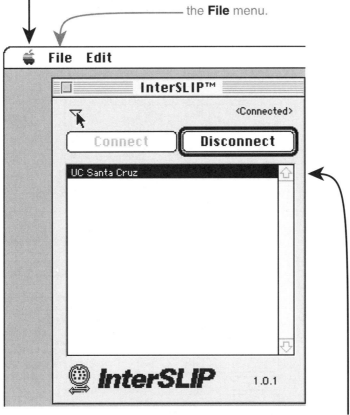

We have supplied one connection file, and its associated "gateway script"

Figure 8-5. *InterSLIP Setup top level window.*

8.6.2 InterSLIP connection scripts

Another plain text file, the *connection* (or *gateway script*), is used to describe the interaction that happens after you have dialed successfully to another computer. In order to automate the login procedure, and to allow **InterSLIP** to request SLIP services from the remote host, your computer and the remote computer must have a conversation. The remote host may ask for a username and

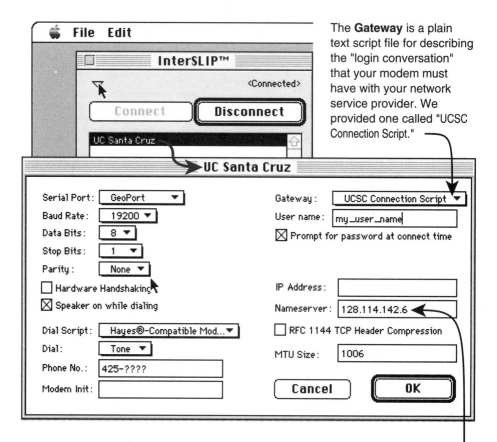

The **Gateway** is a plain text script file for describing the "login conversation" that your modem must have with your network service provider. We provided one called "UCSC Connection Script."

The Nameserver field needs to be filled in before you try to make your first connection. The address of the name-server is a number given to you by your network service provider when you subscribe.

Figure 8-6. *InterSLIP Setup connection entry dialog box.*

password, along with other startup text. There is a special language that must be used inside a connection script. This language is called CCL (Communications Control Language).

It isn't easy to get these scripts to work. The reason it isn't easy has to do with the time involved in making slight changes to the script, redialing, watching what happens, and trying again. You should hound the IAP to develop an ***InterSLIP Connection Script*** that is available online for you to download using your terminal emulator. Meanwhile, patience furthers!

You may want to give your provider a copy of the script we put together for connecting to UCSC. They could use that script as a starting point for their own efforts in getting connected.

8.7 Using PPP instead of SLIP

It may be that your provider will have other software they suggest for supporting your Internet connection. One example of an alternative to SLIP is called PPP (short for Point-to-Point Protocol). There are products similar to **InterSLIP** which use this alternate scheme for connecting to your IAP. They still use a modem, still need dialing scripts, and still need to know things such as the nameserver address. PPP may be easier to use in some circumstances because of its slightly improved mechanism for dynamically establishing a new Internet address for your machine each time you call. Unfortunately, not every provider offers PPP services.

8.8 Insisting on software, support, and access

A provider should offer, as part of their initial setup fee, a package of software and support to get you started. If they don't offer the software themselves, then they should provide an approved list of pieces that you may need. We have tried to supply such a package, but it can't be guaranteed to work in every situation. The struggle to get connected can be daunting, but the rewards are well worth it. Don't let a few evenings of cursing at your computer keep you from taking advantage of the resources of the Internet. After you have managed to establish a SLIP connection, you will find yourself calling in at regular intervals to collect e-mail, check your favorite Web pages, and so on. A busy signal means that your provider's modem lines are all in use. If you have to try more than three times to get connected, then they may be overselling the service. Your provider should be able to guarantee you a reasonable level of accessibility.

8.9 Creating an InterSLIP gateway script

Open up the folder that contains the *InterSLIP Gateway Scripts*. There should be one file there which contains the template script which we use to connect to UCSC. You should use the finder to copy this file to one named for your provider (e.g., *Netcom Connection Script*).

After you have made the copy, you are ready to customize the script. First, try to dial in using the script without modification. If it works, you are set! If it doesn't work, you should consider asking your provider to customize it for you. If you are really dedicated, you may want to use your terminal emulator to dial in and watch the set of messages displayed as you try by hand to issue the SLIP commands on your provider's host. Take careful notes of the text which your provider's machine prints out, and modify the gateway script to look for that text and respond accordingly. It took us about three hours of experimentation to get this script right for UCSC. As Thomas Edison once said, genius is 99 percent perspiration and 1 percent inspiration. We hope this book can help spark that 1 percent; you will have to provide the 99 percent as your investment in the future of the Internet.

InterSLIP File Organization

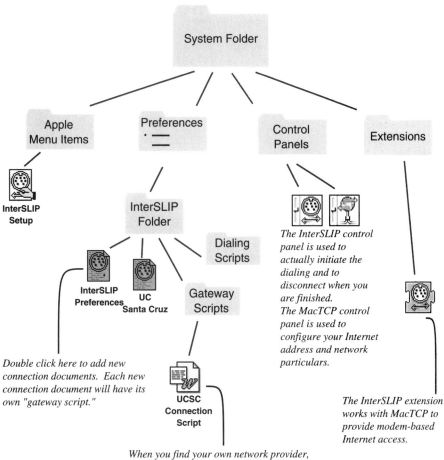

Figure 8-7. *InterSLIP file organization.*

Chapter 9   Windows Bootstrap (Commercial)

Bootstrapping is quite a bit easier with Macintosh than with Windows, so we are going to offer two options here. In this chapter, we survey some commercial (circa $200) connection software. In the next chapter, we give the step-by-step connection guide for the package of nearly free ($20) software we have made available over the Internet. One advantage of the commercial option is the technical support available over the phone from the companies selling the software.

In the October 1994 issue of Internet World, we found three products advertised:

- **Internet In A Box**, from O'Reilly-Spry,
- **Internet Chameleon**, from NetManage, and
- **TCP/Connect II**, from InterCon.

We decided to try all three of these products.[1] The test-bed was a 90 MHz Pentium PC with the latest versions of DOS and Windows, with a serial mouse on port COM1 and an external Hayes-compatible modem on port COM2. Using our University of California dial-up network as a mock Internet provider, we were starting at level 1 with the potential to access either SLIP or PPP at level 2 if we had the right software.

Here are the results of our experiments.

---

1. After going to press, we discovered another such product: PC-SLIP. It is excellent.

9.1 Internet in a Box, aka the Air Series

We called the 800 number given in the advertisement for Spry, and ordered the stand-alone PC version of **Internet-in-a-Box**. Several days later we received a package called the **Spry Air Series 3.0** instead. It turns out that Spry sells several different Internet connectivity packages, and we received a suite of applications that includes **Mosaic**, **Telnet**, **FTP**, **News**, **Gopher**, and other utilities for establishing a PPP connection and taking full advantage of the Internet. It wasn't what we ordered, but it seemed to fill the bill nonetheless.

The installation program is typical of many Windows packages. You start up Windows and choose **Run** from the **File** menu.

```
a:\setup
```

This starts a nicely designed interaction in which the first set of choices depends on whether or not you already have a TCP/IP connectivity package. We were starting from scratch, so we chose to install the **Air Series** and its TCP transport.[2] The next dialog box let us select the range of applications to install. We used the OK button to install everything which took about 4.8 Mb of disk space on our C: drive.

The next dialog box brings up an interesting question that everyone has to decide for any kind of networking software. In most cases the programs that connect your machine to the data provider have a spot for filling in your account name and password to allow a more automated login procedure. This is convenient, but it allows anyone with physical access to your machine to have software access to your Internet account. The **Air Series** can be installed with a more secure scheme that doesn't record the password in a file, which forces you to type it each time you want to connect. We prefer convenience to security and said "no" in answer to the query about using the secure version of the **Air Series**.

The next dialog box asks for an e-mail address. You will probably want to use the account name from your Internet access provider rovider (e.g., myaccount@myprovider.com).

---

2. A TCP transport is another name for a TCP stack, the collection of software layers needed to provide an Internet connection.

The typical TCP-IP support software will have to be configured with IP addresses for each of the machines shown here. The provider should give you these addresses.

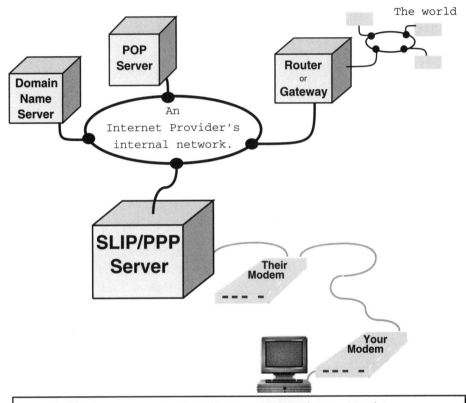

A *domain name server* is a machine whose job is to translate human-style host names into 32 bit internet numbers for all of the other machines connected on its subnet.

A *gateway* or router copies data from your provider's local network segment to a wider area network as necessary.

A *SLIP/PPP server* has a number of modems attached and translates the serial packets from the modems into network packets to provide TCP-IP connectivity.

A *POP server* is a machine whose job is to store e-mail and forward it later to any other machine (namely yours) that connects using TCP-IP and the Post Office Protocol.

Figure 9-1. *Overview of an Internet Access Provider's network.*

At this point we were instructed through a series of disk changes. When the files were done loading we were prompted with a dialog box which asks which of the TCP-transport schemes to install. The choices provide for the use of direct ethernet cards, connecting through Novell and other networks, or dial-up PPP access, which is what we preferred.

After another disk change we were ready to start configuring the PPP connection software. The next dialog box required us to check boxes to indicate which serial port our modem was connected to (COM1 or COM2), what speed to use for the modem, and whether the modem is Hayes-compatible.

Before you try to dial in via modem, you will have to subscribe with an IAP. They should give you:

- modem telephone number (e.g., **408,425,1314**)
- name server address (e.g., **128.114.142.6**)
- domain name (e.g., **ucsc.edu**)

The installation guide from Spry is quite handy in that they provide a Quick Installation Card which lists all of the questions and dialog box entries that you will have to fill in. This way, you can fill in the card once and reproduce the information quickly if something goes wrong. To use the PPP service from your own provider, you will have to modify the phone number, nameserver, domain name, and connection script information in the **Network->Dialer Setup** dialog box of the **Air Dialer** application (see Figure 8-2 on page 82.)

> **Dialer Setup**
>
> **PPP Access Numbers**
>
> Dial Before: [   ]
>
> Phone Number: [425.8930]
>
> **Network Settings**
>
> Your IP Address: [0.0.0.0]
>
> Name Server 1: [128.114.142.6]
>
> Your Host Name: [jrppp.ucsc.edu]
>
> Domain Name: [ucsc.edu]

Figure 9-2. *Dialer Setup dialog for the Air Series from Spry.*

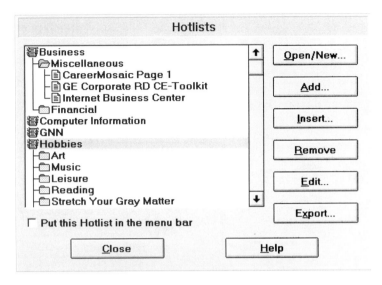

Figure 9-3. *The extensive Air Series jump station is outstanding.*

We found that using the manual login procedure with this product was actually more convenient than trying to figure out the connection script mechanism. As soon as we typed the PPP command to the remote host, the **Dialer** application took over automatically and set up the rest of the connection.

Once again we have managed to reach level 2! One nice thing about the **Air Series** is the fact that it comes with its own version of **Mosaic** and a versatile helper application called **ImageViewer** for displaying side-window graphics, so you get level 2 and level 3 connectivity bundled in the same package.

Another feature we really liked about the Spry package was the extensive jump station already loaded with several categories, and the facility for adding additional entries. It is quite possible that someday Web page hotlists will be a commodity all by themselves. Imagine a complete Webography on disk describing international resources about literary figures, technical subjects, or environmental issues. Compiling these lists and providing them might one day be worth money to software suppliers and would-be users of such lists. Spry's hotlists provided a good sampling of Internet resources.

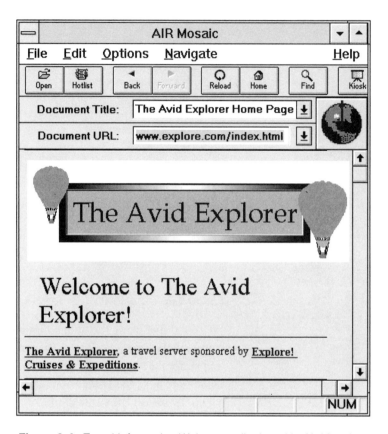

Figure 9-4. *Travel information Web page displayed in Air-Mosaic.*

We did have some problems with the Spry package during a second and third try at installing the package on different machines: slightly inconsistent installation actions and occasional locking up during a **Mosaic** or **Telnet** session. We ended up having to get friendly help from the technical support number printed on the inside jacket of the large book which came with the **Air Series**. Don't be bashful about calling for help. In our case, we actually used another machine already connected to the Internet to download a patch from Spry. The technical support staff walked us through the newly patched installation and things worked fairly smoothly after that.

9.2 Chameleon

This software package is already well known, and is included on a diskette in seven current books on the Internet for Windows users. As these books cost typically about $40, while Chameleon direct from **NetManage** costs $199, we recommend you buy one of the books (see the Bibliography for details).

Another option for trying out Chameleon is to use their 30-day free trial arrangement. Here is how:

- Login to your provider's host using a terminal emulator. We used the Terminal application supplied with Windows under the Accessories workgroup.

- Use ftp to connect with ftp.netmanage.com.

Here is a script of our session:

```
server% ftp ftp.netmanage.com
Connected to netman-gate.netmanage.com.
220 NetManage FTP server sunny (Version 4.14 Thu
Feb 4 12:14:51 PST 1993) ready.
Name (ftp.netmanage.com:claspac): anonymous
331 Guest login ok, send your e-mail address as
password.
Password:will@jri.ucsc.edu
ftp> ls -a
pub
ftp> cd pub
250 CWD command successful.
ftp> ls -a
150 Opening ASCII mode data connection for /bin/
ls.
demos
incoming
outgoing
product_info
readme.txt

ftp> cd demos
ftp> ls -a
```

```
chameleon
sampler
sockwrench
ftp> cd chameleon
ftp> ls -a
chameln1.exe
chameln2.exe
chameln3.exe
chameln4.exe
readme.txt
ftp> mget
(remote-files) *
mget chameln1.exe? y
mget chameln2.exe? y
mget chameln3.exe? y
mget chameln4.exe? y
mget readme.txt? y
ftp> quit
221 Goodbye.
```

mget uses a binary transfer mode automatically on our system. Be sure to check that yours uses a binary transfer.

- Configure the **Terminal** application to use the correct transfer protocol (kermit or xmodem). Use the *Transfer* or *Download* menu to receive a binary file after issuing the send command from the server. The provider should support using kermit or xmodem from the UNIX shell to transfer files to your machine. We used kermit. Be sure to check that the files come across with the same size.

Our script:

```
% kermit -s chameleon1.exe
escape back to your system and give the receive
command
```

- Transfer all four **Chameleon** files to your machine into one directory called **chameln**.

- Execute each of these self-extracting archive files. Just answer "no" to any complaints about overwriting files. We also saw one checksum error as they were unpacking, but it didn't affect the running applications. You will have to experiment if there are transfer errors of this sort.

- After all four archive pieces have been extracted, start up Windows and run the program

  ```
  C:\chameln\setup.exe
  ```

  This program expands files again and creates another directory called **netmanage**. This is where the actual workgroup of programs to run under Windows will live. You can remove the `chameln` directory later.

- When the installation is complete, you will be led through the configuration process. The application is called **Custom**. You will have to create an interface entry by choosing SLIP, PPP, or some other connection type. We used PPP.

- Once you start editing a connection entry, you will have to enter a phone number, *domain name*, and the Internet address of a *nameserver* (all of which you should get from your provider).

- At some point you will have to edit the file.

  ```
  c:\netmanag\slip.ini
  ```

  The support at NetManage, Inc. was excellent for walking me through the process of creating an "expect-send" script.

  With the tech-support folks at NetManage, we were able to get connected after two tries and about 20 minutes of support.

- Connection – Blast Off! Seconds after the PPP connection was established, we launched **Cello** and **voila**, and became level 3 citizens of the Internet.

The **Chameleon** product comes with a news reader, a gopher client, ftp utilities, telnet, and other neat stuff. You still need, for level 3, a WWW browser. We recommend **Cello** or **WinWeb**, which may be obtained via anonymous **ftp** after **Chameleon** is installed and working. The address for downloading a free version of **Cello** is:

```
ftp:/./einet.com:/pc/cello
```

The Chameleon TCP-IP connectivity package from NetManage, Inc. comes with a TCP stack for SLIP or PPP, WINSOCK.DLL, and most of the applications you'll need for level 2.

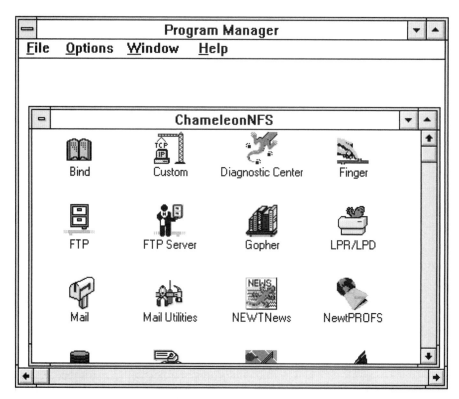

Newt is the network connection monitor; it is active all the while you are connected via PPP.

Figure 9-5. *Files and icons from Chameleon for Windows 3.1.*

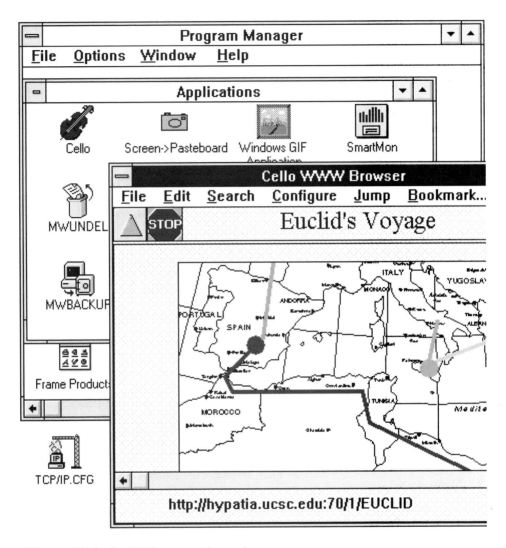

*We established a PPP connection using
Chameleon's "Custom" application, clicked on
Cello to launch it, and it ran immediately.*

Figure 9-6. *An inline graphic shown using Cello with Chameleon.*

9.3 TCP/Connect II

When we called the 800 number given in the *Internet World* advertisement, we received instructions for mgetting the software via anonymous-**ftp** from ftp.intercon.com. This software is a fully functional version of the commercial package, which evaporates in 30 days. We downloaded this to a PC at the university, which is on the Internet, and copied the PKZIPped files to four diskettes.[3] We hand-carried these disks to the test machine and installed them onto its hard disk. After customizing the interface (a few trials were needed), the TCPCONN program started up, but immediately produced a "General Protection Fault" in the library modem.dll. We then called **InterCon** for help, left a message (all helpers were busy), and waited several days for a call back. So we failed to test this package. If you do get it working, however, you still need a separate WWW browser, such as **Cello**, **Mosaic**, or **WinWeb**.

9.4 Buckle down WinSocky

When the Internet was a gleam in the Defense Department's eye, the software functions which supported the network were named.[4] The folks at UC Berkeley decided to call one end of a network connection a *socket*. When a library of routines for supporting the network was finally written for Windows it was called **WinSock**. In order that one standard implementation of this network software can be shared by several different network applications (e.g., **telnet**, **ftp**, **Cello**) the socket functionality is packaged into a *shared library*. The quality of a TCP package for Windows is measured by how well a particular vendor's library adheres to the standards used throughout the industry. Problems increase when you try to mix the software applications from one vendor with the libraries of another. The term *open systems* refers to the effort some companies are making to adhere more strictly to industry standards. This gives the consumer a wider variety of choices in hardware and software vendors, increases competition, and lowers prices. For years, large companies such as IBM, Hewlett Packard, and Microsoft turned

---

3. PKZIP is a compression application.
4. The history of the Internet is summarized nicely in Douglas Comer's more technical book, *Internetworking with TCP/IP.*

their backs on the idea of open systems. The economy in the early 1990s and the volume of computer sales have motivated just about every company to at least pay lip service to the idea, if not the actual implementation, of open systems.

Cello is the name of public domain WWW browsing software that runs under MS-Windows 3.1. It also comes with an Internet e-mail front-end.

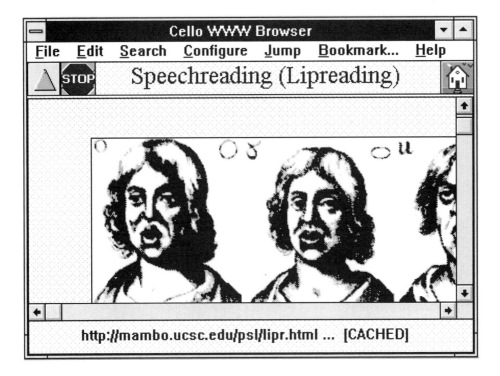

Whether you have a PC or Macintosh or X-Windows platform, every possible topic can be found after a fascinating search through cyberspace. In this example, a Web site at UCSC provides voluminous information about psycho-linguistics and the mechanics of speech.

Figure 9-7. *Cello displaying WWW page on psycho-linguistics.*

9.5 The future of Windows networking

The situation is evolving rapidly, and it is rumored that Windows 95, when it arrives, will offer its own TCP stack, SLIP, and PPP support as standard features. At that point, all you should need is freeware such as Cello or WinWeb, and an Internet SLIP/PPP provider, and you will be able to achieve nirvana at level 3 without giving up all your worldly goods to pay for it!

Chapter 10 Windows Bootstrap (Shareware)

In addition to the commercial software described in the preceding chapter, we examined the shareware configurations of at least four different people who fall into the class of people known as *closet geeks*.[1] All of these folks had spent hours and hours of struggle and rebooted their machines so many times that they couldn't keep track. We will spare you the details of that struggle. With luck we will spare you some of those hours if you read this chapter carefully. But don't be surprised if you have to reboot a few times during the set-up phase.

There is a very inexpensive package that you should be able to get running with patience and a free evening. Called **Trumpet WinSock** by Peter Tattam, it is available as shareware for $20 from many sites on the Internet, including ours.

---

1. Unlike the usual use of the term *closet*, here we actually mean a physical closet. These people are so dedicated to their computers that at any hour of the day or night you could find them holed up in a little room with an eerie blue light reflected from their shining faces. "Coming out of the closet" in this case means squinting into the bright light of day after a long session struggling with their PCs.

10.1 What is a TCP stack?

A TCP stack is a suite of layered software modules. It is called a stack because the pieces are stacked on top of each other and each layer depends on the layer below. A TCP stack provides the low-level software functions used for networking. User-level applications such as **ftp**, **telnet**, and **Mosaic** are written on top of a TCP stack. **Trumpet WinSock** is a shareware implementation of a TCP stack.

A TCP stack generally consists of:

1. A dynamically linked library file called `WINSOCK.DLL`, which must reside in a directory that is part of your *PATH*.

2. An application for helping you set up the initial TCP configuration (in the **Trumpet** package it is called **TCP-Man**: short for TCP Management Application).

3. A set of configuration files and communications control scripts which must be placed in the correct directories.

4. A TSR (Terminate and Stay Resident) program called a packet driver. A packet driver can come in several different flavors to support different networking schemes (the **Trumpet** package has the SLIP packet driver built into **TCP-Man**, so a separate packet driver isn't needed).

The pieces we have described above are all used to build a TCP stack. The hard part about trying to configure DOS and Windows for networking is that the many pieces needed to build a TCP stack come from different vendors, and as a result they don't always fit together the way you'd hoped. Imagine trying to use a Toyota tail light in a Volkswagen car. They both use tail lights, but you can't really expect any compatibility.

All of these pieces have to be assembled with glue, rubber bands, and configuration files as part of the set-up process for getting networked in a DOS/Windows environment.

If there are errors in any of these software layers or any of the configuration files, the whole thing breaks down. The hard part in debugging a network problem with this scheme is finding out which layer or configuration file is at fault.

The tremendous benefit of purchasing a commercial solution such as **Chameleon** is the support you get during this set-up phase. Using the shareware may be cheaper in terms of dollars, but in the long run, the stress and time involved may not be worth the few dollars saved. Our experience led us to conclude that $200 was well worth the improved robustness of the software and the sense of security in knowing there was somewhere to call for help. This help was especially appreciated in writing the dialing and login scripts.

As you follow these instructions, check off each successful step. Go slowly and read everything twice before proceeding and you will ultimately save time. If you skipped the Macintosh chapter, please go back and read sections "Internet addresses" on page 87 and "What is a network gateway?" on page 88.

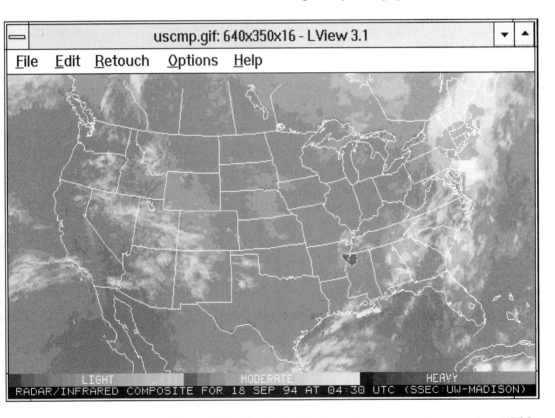

Figure 10-1. *Mosaic for Windows displays a weather map from USGS.*

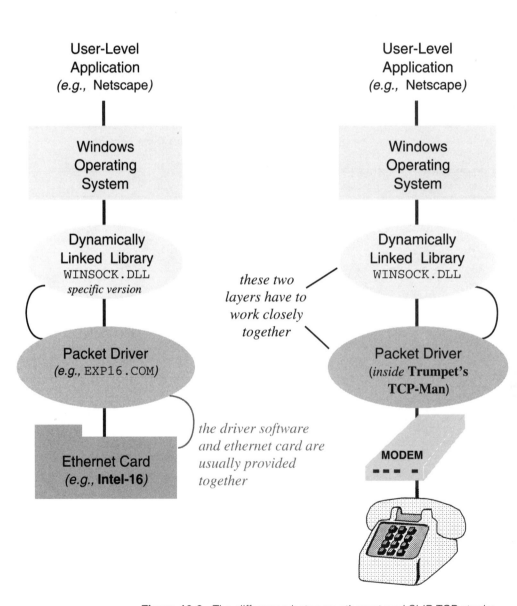

Figure 10-2. *The difference between ethernet and SLIP TCP stacks.*

10.2 Installing Trumpet WinSock

The **Trumpet WinSock** package is a well-known TCP stack which can be found at several *anonymous* **ftp** sites. The term **WinSock** is an abbreviation for Windows Socket Library. The Windows Socket Library, or WINSOCK.DLL, is just one layer in the stack of software needed for connecting a DOS machine to the Internet.

For early explorers of the Internet, finding all of the pieces from the dynamically linked library to the actual user level applications could take hours or weeks. We have packaged all of the pieces together for you in one handy file. Other sites may also offer the **Trumpet WinSock** package but it may be configured differently at different locations. The package described below was found at

```
ftp://jri.ucsc.edu/natsci/software/
       dos/network/netdos.zip
```

To obtain this package:

- Login to your provider's host using a terminal emulator. We used the **Terminal** application supplied with Windows under the Accessories workgroup.

- Use **ftp** from your provider's host to connect with our site at jri.ucsc.edu.

This is a script of our session:

```
server% ftp jri.ucsc.edu
Connected to jri.ucsc.edu.
Name (jri.ucsc.edu:claspac): anonymous
331 Guest login ok, send ident as password.
Password: you@yourhost.yourdomain
ftp> ls -aCF
./                      greeting.txt        prod-
ucts/
../                     imagemap.conf       read-
me.ftp
.cache                  images/             rec-
ipes.html
arts/                   include/            sam-
ple_table.html
```

*The **-aCF** options to **ls** make for easier reading of the listing.*

```
bin/                    incoming/
sounds/
cgi-bin/                jrclass/
unex/
dwh/                    map.default.html
webmaster/
etc/                    menu               web-
start.html
gn_docs/                natsci/

ftp> cd natsci
250 CWD command successful.
ftp> cd software
250 CWD command successful.
ftp> cd dos
250 CWD command successful.
ftp> ls -aCF
./              ../         convenience/
menu        network/
ftp> cd convenience
ftp> ls -aCF
./              instpro.txt   pkunzip.exe
uncompre.exe
../             menu          snapshot.exe
uudecode.exe
.cache          mksdupe.zip   tar.exe
```

*The **binary** command is essential to transfer files of this type.*

```
ftp> binary
200 Type set to I.
ftp> get pkunzip.exe
150 Opening BINARY mode for pkunzip.exe
(29378 bytes).
226 Transfer complete.
29378 bytes received in 0.14 seconds (2e+02
Kbytes/s)
ftp> cd ../network
```

```
250 CWD command successful.
ftp> ls -aCF
./              cats14k.cmd    cello.zip
netdos.zip
../             cats9600.cmd   menu
netscape.zip

ftp> get netdos.zip
150 Opening BINARY mode for netdos.zip
(1286678 bytes).
226 Transfer complete.
1286678 bytes received in 3.82 seconds
(3.2e+02 Kbytes/s)
ftp> quit
221 Goodbye.
```

- Configure the **Terminal** application to use the correct transfer protocol (kermit or xmodem). Use the *Transfer* or *Download* menu to receive a binary file after issuing the send command from your provider's host. Your Internet provider should support using **kermit** or **xmodem** from the UNIX shell to transfer files to your machine. We used **kermit**. Be sure to check that the files come across with the same size.

```
% kermit -i -s netdos.zip
escape back to your system and give the
receive command
```

Using the Windows **Terminal** application on your own machine, pull down the *Transfers* menu and select the *Receive Binary File* option. This should prompt you for the file name you want to create on your local drive; we chose C:\netdos.zip. You should consider making a floppy with this single file on it labeling it "Internet Starter Kit Install Disk."

This floppy disk will serve as a backup in case something goes wrong during the installation. Take our word for it: keep a copy on floppies as well as your hard drive.

Repeat the download procedure for the pkunzip.exe file if you don't already have that on your computer.

```
% kermit -i -s pkunzip.exe
```
escape back to your system and give the
receive command

- Leave the **Terminal** application and exit from Windows. At the
  DOS prompt give these commands:
  ```
  C:> cd \
  C:> pkunzip -d netdos.zip
  ```
- At this point you should have a directory called C:\TEMPDOS
  that contains the installation program for our Internet Kit.
- After unzipping the Internet Kit give the commands:
  ```
  C:> cd c:\tempdos
  C:> install
  ```
- Use the return key to skip over the default pathnames for each of
  the packages.
- Hit return when it asks you to confirm the pathnames.

The install program launches **pkunzip** to unpack a bunch of new
programs and configuration files onto your hard disk. **pkunzip**
may complain if it finds you have already done an installation or
some files already exist. Usually it is safe to answer **y** in response
to these overwrite warnings.

- After the directories have been created the installer will ask you if
  you want your AUTOEXEC.BAT and CONFIG.SYS automatically modified. Just say yes.

10.3 Adding a new Windows workgroup

- Reboot and then start up Windows.
- Pull down the *File* menu and select *New* and then "Program
  Group."
- A window appears into which you must type a descriptive name
  and the complete pathname of the group file we supplied with your
  Internet kit.

  Description: `Internet` *<tab>*

  Group File: `C:\netwin\internet.grp`

- You will know that everything has worked so far if a new group called **Internet** appears on your desktop.
- Edit the file called C:\trumpet\login.cmd. Examine the interactions described in this script file. We will show you ours below. You will have to change the input and output instructions to match the conversation your particular network provider's machine will be expecting. If possible, find someone else who already has it working. Call your provider to see if they have working login scripts for **Trumpet WinSock**. We also provide samples for connecting to UCSC's SLIP service as a starting point which you will find on the disk after doing the installation. These files end in a ".cmd" suffix.

Writing the login script is the toughest part of the installation. You should decide on an Internet provider based in part on their willingness to help you write these dial-in scripts.

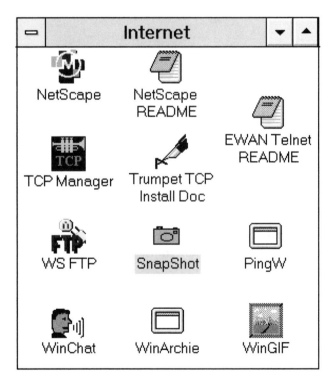

Figure 10-3. We added an Internet work-group for WWW software.

10.4 Sample Trumpet WinSock connection script

*The CCL command **output** sends any following text to the modem or remote host.*

```
# file: C:\trumpet\login.cmd
# initialize modem
#
output atz\13
input 10 OK\n
#
# set modem to indicate DCD
#
output at&f&c1&d2\13
input 10 OK\n
#
# send phone number
#
output atdt4258948\13
#
# now we are connected.
#
input 30 CONNECT
#
#  wait until safe to send because some
modems hang up
#  if you transmit during the connection
phase
#
wait 30 dcd
#
#  get UCSC banner.  ask for SLIP connection
#  give username and password for authenti-
cation
#
input 30 comm-tsa, modem
output slip\13
input 30 Username:
```

*The **input** command waits a few seconds before expecting to see the exact text shown.*

*The **\13** and other backslash sequences are sent as carriage returns and other special characters to the modem or remote host.*

<table>
<tr><td>

*The CCL command **username** brings up a dialog box at this point during the execution.*

*The **\u** will be replaced with the value entered into that box.*

*The **address** command expects a valid 32-bit Internet address is ready to read from the remote host.*

</td><td>

```
username Enter your username
output \u\13
input 30 Password:
password Enter your password
output \p\13
#
#get IP address for winsock
#
input 30 Your address is
address 30
input 30 \n
display \n
display Connected.  Your IP address is \i.\n
```

</td></tr>
</table>

10.5 Configuring TCP-Man

- The installer should have modified your `autoexec.bat` file to add the `trumpet` directory to your PATH. Here is what ours looks like:

  PATH=**C:\TRUMPET;**C:\DOS;C:\BIN;

  After confirming that your `autoexec.bat` file has the new path correctly set, you are ready to reboot and fire up Windows.

- We double-clicked on the TCP Management program and it brought up a dialog box in which we had to fill in the following items:

  1. The 32-bit IP address of the name and time servers (e.g., **128.114.142.6**).

  2. The domain suffix (e.g., *ucsc.edu*).

  3. An *X* should appear in the box for **Internal SLIP.**

  4. Remove the *X* that may come up for **Hardware Handshake**.

  5. The SLIP port number should be 1 or 2, depending on which serial port your modem is connected to.

6. The baud rate should be set to the highest speed your modem can handle (e.g., 2400-19200.)

- Now you must reboot again and restart Windows. At this point (and after every failed attempt to connect) you should turn the modem off, then back on, reboot, and restart Windows. We had to reboot a dozen times before managing to connect.

- Relaunch the **TCP-Man** application. Pull down the *Dial* menu and select *Login*.

- Watch the interaction as your `login.cmd` script is executing. If all goes well, you should have to enter a username and password and finally you will see a message saying `SLIP enabled`.

- Miniaturize the **TCP-Man** application and double-click on the **Netscape** icon. Don't be surprised if it fails the first time, with a message `DNS lookup failed`. This could be a real error (e.g., you entered the nameserver's address incorrectly) or a spurious error resulting from the start of a new connection.

- Pull down the **Netscape** *File* menu. Select *Open Location*.

- Enter the full path of your favorite URL and hit return. We used: `http://jri.ucsc.edu`

- Connection – Blast Off! Ten hours after starting this SLIP installation we were able to launch **Netscape** and become level 3 citizens of the Internet all over again.

Trumpet WinSock File Organization

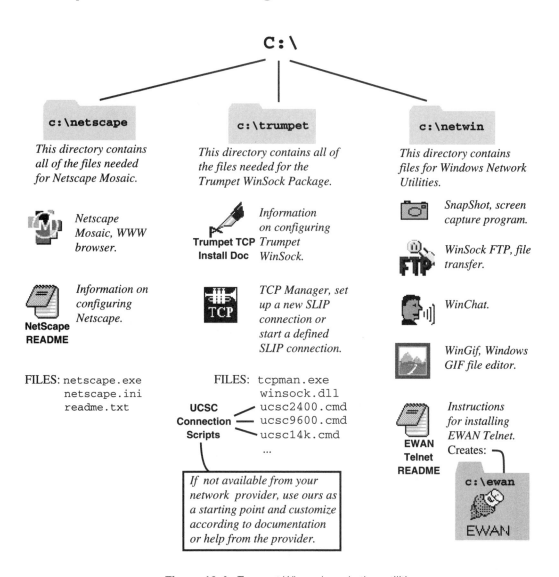

Figure 10-4. *Trumpet Winsock and other utilities.*

10.6 Configuring Netscape

The Netscape browser has a nicer configuration interface than either Mosaic or Cello. After starting Netscape, pull down the **Options** menu and select **Preferences**.

There are several nicely laid out screens to use. The most important box to fill in is the Home Page box on the **Style** screen.

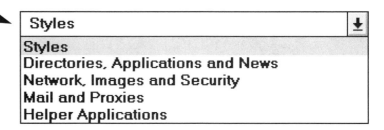

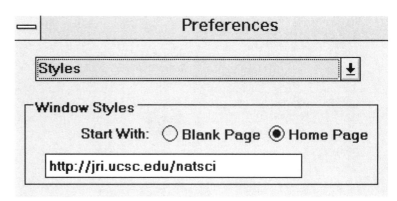

Figure 10-5. *Netscape Styles screen from Preferences.*

10.7 32-bit computing with Windows

Until Windows-95 is available and stable, some programs that need 32-bit computing will use a special library or program called `win32s`. If the software developers are careful, they can simulate 32-bit operations using this package. Some versions of the network and browsing software require that you load `win32s` before you use them. A commercial product which requires `win32s` will generally provide it for you. Public domain software packages with bundles of 32-bit software should come with it also. A free version can be obtained from Microsoft at the URL:

```
ftp://ftp.microsoft.com/developr/win32dk/
sdk-public
```

10.8 Can you see through Windoze?

After reading through the preceding pages of shareware installation instructions, we think you'll agree that using a commercial product such as **Chameleon** is definitely worthwhile because you have somewhere to turn if you have problems along the way. The shareware and freeware doesn't come with that support.

In favor of Windows, all we can say is: we hope a future version of Windows is more convenient for WWW citizenship!

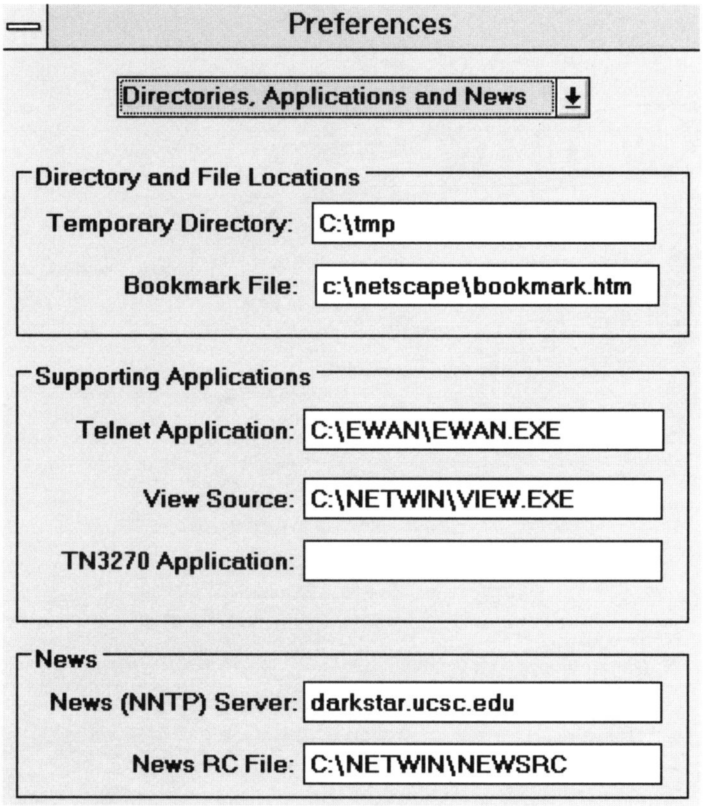

Figure 10-6. *Netscape directories screen from Preferences.*

Part 3   # Beginning UNIX

Perhaps you will achieve full WWW citizenship without ever encountering UNIX. That has been the case for many new citizens of the WWW. However, if you must truly bootstrap yourself all the way from level 0 to level 3, and you do not wish to buy commercial software as a short cut, you will need UNIX literacy at the crucial step at which you use the UNIX command **ftp** to copy software from somewhere on the Internet to your Internet access providers machine, and then download it to your own machine.

Furthermore, UNIX is wonderful, and essential for true computer literacy. So for business or pleasure, here is a very concise beginner's guide to the underworld of the Internet.

Chapter 11   UNIX Basics

11.1 What is UNIX?

UNIX is a trademark name for a multiuser multitasking operating system developed at AT&T over 25 years ago. It was designed as a general purpose computing environment. As with any software product, the more general the software, the harder it is to learn and apply to some specific task. Advocates of UNIX will tell you that the power and flexibility of UNIX are worth the steep learning curve. Casual computer users will probably disagree.

11.1.1 UNIX: The expert friendly operating system

Most software is sold on the premise that it is *user friendly*. This expression usually refers to the fact that the learning curve for a user friendly piece of software lets the user get started with a minimum of experience. *Expert friendly* software is a term we use to describe software that has a steep learning curve, but which provides power and flexibility for doing complex operations with a minimum of typing. This expert friendly notion is pervasive throughout UNIX, and as a result many perspective UNIX users are driven away before they really get started. This text is not intended to get you over this steep learning curve by itself. We hope that you will use this brief introduction to UNIX as a starting point for your further exploration.

11.1.2 What is an operating system?

An operating system is a combination of the binary instructions permanently stored in the ROM of your computer and other software instructions which are loaded off a disk when you boot up the machine. This master program, the one which runs all the time and which **invokes** the other programs, is the operating system.

The operating system's job is to provide low-level mini programs or routines to access the disk drives, tape drives, printer ports, and to start up jobs or other programs that use those resources.

11.1.3 Difference between UNIX and other operating systems

UNIX is *both* an operating system and computing environment. For years if you bought a PC or Macintosh, you would find those machines virtually unusable until you loaded them up with your favorite applications. Recently vendors have begun to supply preinstalled packages with word processing, database, and drawing applications.

When people use a UNIX machine, they can be sure not only that the machine will boot up and be running UNIX, the low-level operating system, but that they will also be supplied with hundreds of programs to perform the operations listed above and more.

11.1.4 Some DOS improvements taken from UNIX

- Directories, hierarchical file system
- PATH searches for executables
- PROMPT and other "shell" variables

11.2 Advantages of UNIX

Early on, UNIX became the network operating system of choice, with TCP/IP embedded within it. The Internet evolved with the idea of connecting UNIX hosts worldwide.

11.2.1 Some of its strengths

- E-mail is a standard UNIX utility, and the configuration necessary for e-mail transfer via modem (USENET) or the Internet is supplied with most machines.

- All UNIX machines provide a nearly identical working environment.

- Most programs are portable from one UNIX machine to another, if source code is available.

- UNIX machines run many programs simultaneously. The programs can be run in the background to do useful work without interfering with your screen.

- Most UNIX machines have virtual memory, which removes any upper limit on the amount of memory a program can use.

- UNIX allows shared access to the same data, with controls on who can read or write shared files.

- Online documentation for every program and maintenance procedure greatly reduces office clutter and the huge task of maintaining up-to-date user manuals on paper.

- As an operating system and a set of methods for performing backups, few other systems can match UNIX for reliability.

11.2.2 UNIX: software development

The task for which UNIX is best suited is software development. Virtual memory and other low-level memory protection schemes make it virtually impossible to crash a UNIX machine by accident. Thus, software development is greatly accelerated. The availability of C, C++, Objective C, Pascal, Fortran, and a host of CAD and database language tools make UNIX an excellent choice for any new development effort.

11.3 Disadvantages of UNIX

A general purpose tool can be both a good and bad thing: good because of its flexibility and adaptability to a wide range of problems, bad because it may not specialize or excel at any one task. Here are some of its specific weaknesses.

11.3.1 Expense

Up until recently, machines that could run UNIX were more expensive than most small businesses or individuals could afford. Therefore, commercial vendors of software products for small businesses and individuals have ignored UNIX as a platform for their products. Even today, there are no widely accepted UNIX-based spreadsheet programs or easy-to-use database programs, no widely accepted applications for supporting retail sales, video-store management, and so on.

As the price of UNIX machines comes within reach of small businesses and individuals, these products will become available and the power and capability of the products will benefit from the features which UNIX has to offer.

11.3.2 System administration requirements

UNIX was originally designed to be the operating system for machines which would handle multiple users. One of those users was assumed to be the *system administrator* or *super-user*. The super-user would be in charge of adding and deleting other users' account information and data files, booting up the machine, making backups, and so forth.

Hiring a system administrator is one of the larger costs associated with a UNIX installation. New versions of UNIX are just now appearing for machines which don't assume that there is an expert around to be the super-user.

SCO UNIX, Microsoft XENIX, NeXTStep, and AT&T personal systems are all meant to be used on machines which don't have a full-time system administrator. Several public domain versions of UNIX such as LINUX and GNUNIX are popular among our more technically advanced and thrifty students.

11.4 Logging in

Every UNIX machine has a file called the password file. In the password file are listed all of the valid users, their login names, encrypted versions of their passwords, their real names, where their files live on the system and what program they will start out using when they login. In order for you to login, the system administrator (super-user) had to make an entry in this file for you.

11.4.1 Login steps

The UNIX machine must be powered up and connected to the terminal or computer you are using. The connection to your terminal or PC may be through a modem or a directly connected wire. If you are connected to a UNIX machine from your PC at home through a modem, you are probably using something called a terminal emulator. A terminal emulator is a program which makes your PC behave as if it were an old fashioned terminal. For years, **kermit** was the most popular public domain terminal emulator.

One UNIX machine can serve between 10 and 50 users at a time. A UNIX time-sharing business is one that offers dial-in terminal sessions on their UNIX machine. Every terminal properly connected to the UNIX machine should get a "Login:" prompt.

`Login:` **username**

`Password:` ***your password***   *your password will not be shown as you type.*

Message of the Day...

`You have mail.`   *this prints only if you have mail from someone.*

`TERM = (adm3a)`   *most UNIX machines have terminals connected, what kind is this one?*

`%`   *the C-shell prompt. Here is where you can type UNIX commands.*

11.4.2 Setting up your environment

When you log in, the program you begin executing immediately is called the *shell*. The shell is responsible for interpreting (parsing) the commands you type and for launching the programs which correspond to those commands.

Some programs (like the editor) need to know what kind of terminal you are using so that they know how to clear the screen and move the cursor around. The shell has a startup file called **.login** (sort of equivalent to the DOS file AUTOEXEC.BAT) which contains the text for commands to ask you to identify your terminal type and other start up instructions.

11.4.3 The login shell

The shell is just one of the hundreds of programs available to use with UNIX. Like any other program, it comes as a file on the disk. There are several different shells available under UNIX. The oldest version of the shell is called the Bourne Shell after the man who wrote it. A newer version of the shell is called the C-Shell. This version of the UNIX shell was written at UC Berkeley.

The shell has the following basic job:

- Print a prompt.
- Read a line of text from the user.
- If the line of text starts with the name of an executable file, launch that file and wait for it to finish.

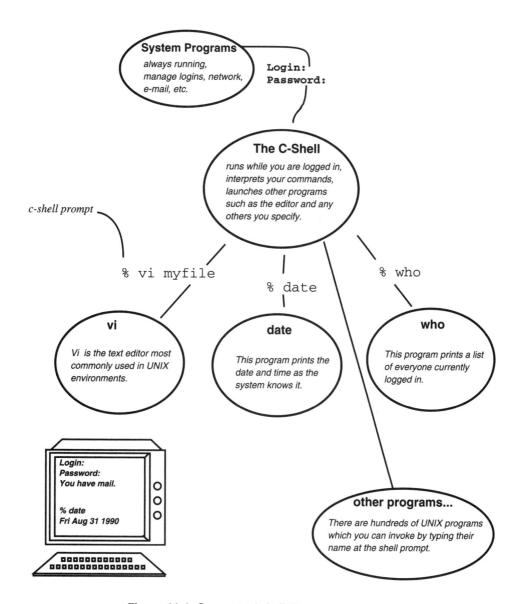

Figure 11-1. *Conceptual shell diagram.*

11.5 Documentation conventions

The C-Shell prints the percent sign as its ordinary prompt. When-ever you see the notation % *command*, it means that you should type the word command as a C-Shell command. Other programs in UNIX have different prompts. When you see these other prompts in documentation such as

    $ command

or

    A> command

then you know that the documentation is referring to the command in some other context. In this case, the dollar sign is the Bourne Shell prompt and the **A>** is the DOS prompt.

11.6 Simple commands

Try each of these:

```
% who
% whoami
% cal
% ls
% ls -a
% passwd
% set history 10
% history
% logout
```

11.6.1 Command formats

Almost every shell command has roughly the same format. Each command is made up of a space-separated list of words. The first word of every command is the program name. For the command % **ls,** the one and only word on the command line is the program name.

Most UNIX programs have alternate behaviors which are triggered by *command line flags*. The **ls** program recognizes several flags.

Most programs expect one or more single-letter flags, which are recognized by a preceding dash or minus sign.

The command % **ls -a** is read aloud as: *L S dash A*.

The **-a** flag tells the **ls** program to modify its task of listing files to include all files. Ordinarily, files whose names begin with a dot are not listed. This allows the creation of *hidden* files which we can usually ignore.

Every word on a command line is called an *argument*. Almost all UNIX commands take arguments of some kind. The **ls** program takes flag arguments and filename arguments. If no filename arguments are passed to the **ls** command, then all the files in the current directory are listed.

11.6.2 More UNIX commands

Try these:

```
% cat .login
% echo "Hello" > README
% more README
% mv README temp       rename the README file
% ls -a
% mv temp README       rename it back to README
```

11.6.3 Control characters

Ordinarily, typing characters from the keyboard causes lower-case letters to be sent from the terminal to the computer. Holding down the shift key and typing characters causes the upper- case letters and other special alternate characters to be sent to the computer.

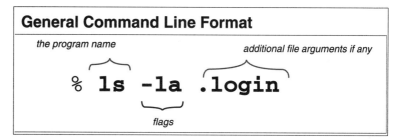

General Command Line Format

the program name

additional file arguments if any

% **ls -la .login**

flags

Figure 11-2. *Command line format.*

Control characters are just one more set of alternate characters on your keyboard. They work just like capital (shifted) letters work. Hold down the control key and then type some letter.

```
Operation       Keystroke   Abbreviation

=========       =========   ============

Backspace       Ctrl-H      ^H
Kill Word       Ctrl-W      ^W
Kill Line       Ctrl-X      ^X
Interrupt       Ctrl-C      ^C
End of File     Ctrl-D      ^D
```

UNIX allows you to pick which control character will perform each of the operations mentioned above. The control characters shown are the usual choices for each operation.

11.7 The UNIX tool box

A complete UNIX system includes a very large software toolbox with programs for doing just about anything you could ask. The consistency of the design for all these programs doesn't quite live up to the standard which the Macintosh has achieved, but there are some things you can generally count on:

*   All programs will be invoked in a similar way
*   Dash arguments are used to change operating flags
*   Output is redirectable to files
*   Input is redirectable from files
*   Files and Devices are treated the same
*   98 percent of the programs you'll use come with and are supported with the operating system
*   Text editing
*   Document formatting
*   Data base systems
*   Compilers
*   Disk, tape, and printer managers
*   File manipulation

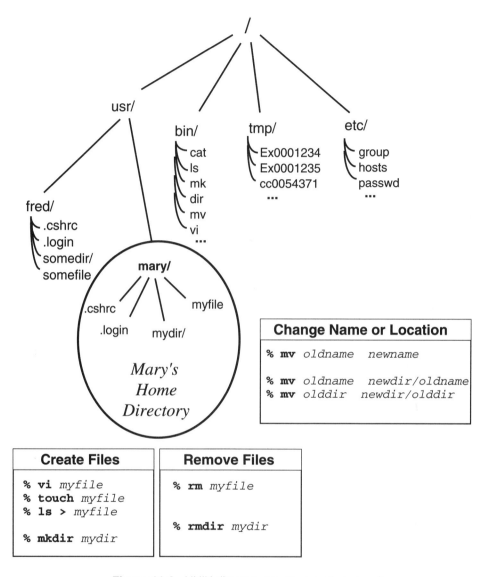

Figure 11-3. *UNIX directory structure and startup files.*

11.8 The online manual

Try this:

```
% man mv
```

Every UNIX machine comes with an online copy of the UNIX reference manual. In addition to descriptions of every UNIX command, the manual is broken into several sections:

```
Section 1          UNIX commands
Section 2          C system calls
Section 3          C, Fortran, Pascal
                   functions
Section 4          Administrative level
                   routines
Section 5          System Administration
Section 6          Games
Section 7          Miscellaneous
Section 8          System Administration
                   (cont.)
```

11.8.1 The online index

Now try this:

```
% man -k "list"      find all the programs which list things
```

Most versions of UNIX support the index search of the manual with this command. Some versions of UNIX don't have this option to the man program. This is an important criterion for evaluating the quality of a UNIX system.

One of the nicest versions of UNIX we have seen is called NeXT-STEP from Steve Jobs's company, NeXT. It runs on a range of hardware platforms, including 486 Intel machines. NeXT's online documentation and indexing system are truly amazing.

In our experience, when you choose an operating system for your computer, you should pick the very best. You'll spend years learning and working with this tool. Since every other program on the machine depends on the operating system, you don't want that investment to be frustrating from the start.

.login

```
setenv PATH "/bin:/usr/bin:/usr/ucb"
set history=22
set noglob;
eval `tset ?adm3a`
unset noglob;
```

The .cshrc *and* .login *files are
"sourced" automatically by the
shell when you login. The commands in
them are executed as if you had typed them
from the keyboard. They don't show up with
* ls *because they begin with a dot.*

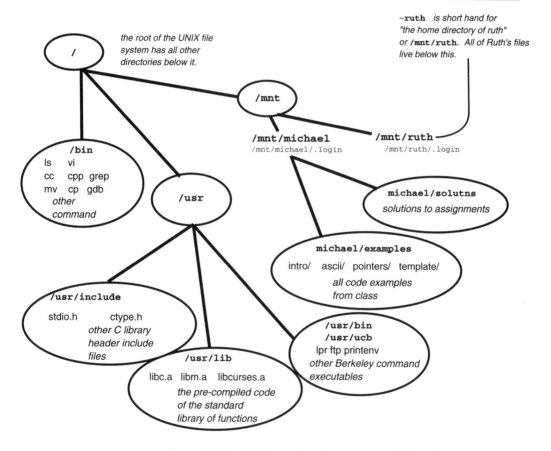

~**ruth** *is short hand for
"the home directory of ruth"
or /***mnt***/***ruth***. All of Ruth's files
live below this.*

*the root of the UNIX file
system has all other
directories below it.*

/

/mnt

/mnt/michael
/mnt/michael/.login

/mnt/ruth
/mnt/ruth/.login

/bin
ls   vi
cc   cpp grep
mv   cp   gdb
*other
command*

/usr

michael/solutns
solutions to assignments

michael/examples
intro/   ascii/   pointers/   template/
*all code examples
from class*

/usr/include
stdio.h   ctype.h
*other C library
header include
files*

/usr/bin
/usr/ucb
lpr ftp printenv
*other Berkeley command
executables*

/usr/lib
libc.a libm.a libcurses.a
*the pre-compiled code
of the standard
library of functions*

Figure 11-4. *UNIX directory structure and startup files.*

Chapter 12   Files and Directories

12.1 The UNIX file system

The UNIX file system is similar to those of DOS and the Macintosh desktop.

12.1.1 Files

One job of an operating system is to provide access to data stored on disks and tapes. Most operating systems provide a way to logically group related data into *files*. A file has a name and may contain text, machine instructions, images, or specially coded binary data for different programs.

12.1.2 Directories

In order to organize large numbers of files into manageable pieces, most operating systems provide a folder or *directory*. This is a logical place to put other files. Each time you enter the command % **ls** you are listing the files in the current directory. When you login, the current directory is automatically set to be your *home directory*. Each user has a personal home directory.

12.1.3 Plain text

Any file you create using the **vi** editor is a plain text file. These are also referred to as ASCII files.

12.1.4 Hidden files

By convention, filenames which start with a dot are not listed by the command **ls**. Some common ones are:

```
.cshrc
.login
.logout
.exrc
```

These files contain housekeeping information and preference settings that rarely need updating.

12.1.5 Executable files

Programs are called *executable files* because they can be executed by typing their name as a command to the shell. Executable files are usually not ASCII files and they cannot be edited using **vi**. In addition to the usual binary executable files, there are plain text files which can be executed as programs. These are called scripts or shell scripts, they have lines of text which work as shell commands.

12.2 The file hierarchy

12.2.1 Moving about

The % **cd** command is used to *change directory*. The shell recognizes this built-in command, and switches you from the directory in which you are working to another in which you want to work (your *current working directory*).

Command	Effect
=======	======
% **cd**	Changes the current working directory to the home directory of the current user
% **cd /**	Changes the current working directory to the root of the hierarchy

% **cd** *dirname*	Changes working directory to dirname
% **cd ..**	Moves closer to the root by one step (up one directory to parent)
% **pwd**	Prints the name of the working directory

12.2.2 Distinguishing different kinds of files

When looking at a list of files and directories, it is hard to tell which are the files and which are the directories. The % **ls** command has a special flag option to help you distinguish between different kinds of files. The command % **ls -F** will cause all directories to be listed with a trailing slash character (even though the slash is not part of the name), and all executable files with a trailing star. From now on we will use these symbols to indicate the type of files we are talking about. Remember that these special symbols are not really part of the file or directory names.

12.3 Filenaming conventions

Without icons to help identify the kind of files you have, a stricter set of naming conventions must be applied. One of the typical directory names you will often see is **bin/**. This is short for *binary* and is typically a directory that contains executable files. Most of the original programs which came with UNIX live in the absolute path **/bin**.

12.3.1 Dot extensions

Most files have some kind of dot ending or suffix that indicates their use. For example: data base files might end in **.db** as in:

```
temp.db
checks.db
transactions.db
```

12.3.2 Good filenaming habits

For every program you use frequently, you should develop a file naming convention for files that go with that program. Typesetters using UNIX, for example, use a program called **troff** or its plain text partner **nroff**. They name their source files with the **.rs** extension to indicate that they are to be used with either **nroff** or **troff**. Filenaming consistency and descriptive names will save hours of work and hunting for files.

12.3.3 Filename length and restrictions

In theory, a UNIX filename can be quite long and can have almost any characters in it. In practice, it is a good idea to limit filenames to 14 to 20 characters. Also, it is safest to stick to letters, numbers and underscores for filenames.

12.4 Copy and move commands

12.4.1 Files to files

The move and copy commands, **mv** and **cp**, work two ways. Applied to files only, they may use two arguments.

> **% cp origfile newfile**

Using two filenames as arguments, **cp** copies the file named in the first argument onto the file named by its second file argument. If the second argument already exists it will be overwritten. The move command is similar.

> **% mv oldname newname**

Using two file names as arguments, **mv** changes the name of its first argument to be the second argument. If there was already a file by the new name it will be overwritten (clobbered).

12.4.2 Files into directories

If the last argument is a directory these commands work differently. Using a list of files as arguments, and a directory as the last argument, as for example,

```
% cp file1 file2 directory
```

cp puts a copy of each file listed into the directory specified. The new files have the same names in the result directory as the old ones did where they lived. Similarly, using a list of files and a directory as the last argument,

```
% mv file1 file2 directory
```

moves each file into the directory specified.

12.4.3 Copying directory hierarchies

It is often the case that you work on a new project that is an updated version of something you have done before. If you have a directory of all the files used for a project together, you can make a new copy of everything using the command:

```
% cp -r paper newpaper
```

12.5 Permissions

For every file on UNIX, there is extra information about the file kept by the operating system on the disk. These extra bytes of information indicate the owner of the file, when the file was last modified, and so on.

12.5.1 Long listings: detailed information on files

The % **ls** command recognizes another flag option to print out more detailed information about files.

```
Permission    Owner    Size  Time          Name
Bits                         Modified
===========   =======  ==    =========     =====
-rw-r--r-- 1  claspac  6118  Jun 13 12:29
intro2.rs
-rwxr-xr-x 1  claspac  11433 Jun 13 12:14  myprog
drwxr-x--- 2  claspac  1024  Aug 10 16:48  labwork/
```

The text above, called a *long listing*, was the result of invoking the command % **ls -l**.

12.5.2 The permission codes

Three bytes of this extra information contain the *permission bits*. The initial d in the left-hand column (the permission section) of the long listing tells you that this entry is a directory.

User	Group	Other	Format
====	=====	=====	=====
rwx	r-x	r-x	*Mode*
111	101	101	*Binary*
7	5	5	*Octal*

The permission bits or *mode* of a file can be changed using the % **chmod** command (see below).

12.5.3 File permissions

File permissions control reading, writing, and executing. The permission modes distinguish three different groups of people: the *owner* of the file, the users in the same *group* as the owner, and all *other users*.

A file is *readable* if someone can use a program like **more** or **vi** to look at the text or contents of the file. This doesn't mean that they can modify it in any way; they can only look.

A file is *writable* if someone can use a program such as **vi** or another utility to modify the text or contents of the file. Ordinarily we keep files writable only by the *owner,* so that other users on the system can't damage or delete text from them.

A file is *executable* if you can issue its filename as a command, and have the system try to execute the instructions contained in that file. Usually only programmers and system administrators add the executable permission to files.

12.5.4 Directory permissions

A directory is *readable* if someone can use a program such as **ls** to see the list of files which is in that directory. They can "read" the directory. They can not modify it in any way.

A directory is *writable* if someone can use a program such as **rm** or another utility to add or remove files from that directory. Ordinarily we keep directories writable only by the owner,so that other users on the system can not remove files.

A directory is *executable* if you can use the command **cd** to change the current working directory in it. Only directories which have the executable bit set can be entered with the command **cd**.

12.6 The chmod **command**

Permission modes on files and directories are changed using the command **chmod**.. It symbolizes the categories of users and per- mission modes by the letters:

u	*user*
g	*group*
o	*all others*
r	*readable*
w	*writable*
x	*executable*

Using these letters, we could set the permission of a file as follows:

```
% chmod ug=rw,o=r myfile
```

If we then obtained a long listing of this file we would see the per- missions:

```
-rw-rw-r-- 2 claspac 1024  Aug 10 16:48 myfile
```

Chapter 13 **E-Mail**

13.1 The UNIX `mail` program

13.1.1 Why e-mail?

Almost 80 percent of all administrative tasks involve shipping data
from one place to another with some small conversion process in
between. In today's offices, most of that information is on both
paper and a computer.

Document preparation tools, databases, and spreadsheets keep letters, payroll, and accounting systems running online, while product
orders, responses to inquiries, and checks may be mostly on paper.
Electronic mail systems can eliminate the need for some of that
paper and speed up transactions.

13.1.2 Benefits of e-mail

For an organization with computers or terminals on most desks,
e-mail allows messages to many departments as easily as to one.
Also, messages can be kept in an online *mail box,* which can provide an easy way to keep track of tasks which may need to be per-
formed.

13.2 Introduction to e-mail addresses

The first e-mail ran under UNIX and most e-mail is still sent
between UNIX systems. In order to use Internet-based electronic

mail you must have a uniquely named host. All Internet hosts have unique names, for example:

```
jri.ucsc.edu
```

Each host may have multiple users, for example:

```
jennifer karino fred
```

UNIX users have account names that are unique *only* on their machines: `jim` on `jri.ucsc.edu` is not necessarily the same as `jim` on `etlport.etl.go.jp`.

Internet e-mail addresses combine account names and machine names together to form an address unique throughout cyberspace

```
jimmy@host.ucsc.edu
jennifer@etlport.etl.go.jp
watson@scilibx.ucb.edu
```

When you login to a UNIX account you might get a message that looks like:

```
You have mail
```

so you may give the command % **mail** to read your mail, which will result in the screen:

```
Mail version 5.2 6/21/85. Type ? for help.
"/usr/spool/mail/claspac":1 message 1
unread
>U 1 carmen@host.ucsc.edu Tue Dec 6 13:42

    &
```

At the mail prompt & type **q** to quit. To send an e-mail message, type at the UNIX prompt, for example:

```
% mail carmen@host.ucsc.edu
   Subject: your letter
   ‡
```

Now you could enter the text of the letter or import a previously prepared file.

13.3 Receiving e-mail

After you have used the command `% mail` you may use the following commands at the mail prompt, &, followed by a return:

To examine message headings:

& **h**	*to look at mail headings*
& *17*	*to look at message 17*

To delete unwanted messages:

& **d**	*to delete the current message*
& **d 1**	*to delete message 1*
& **d 3 5**	*to delete messages 3 and 5*

To save messages to a folder file:

& **s** *1*	**filename**
	to save message 1 in your current working directory
& **s** *1*	**+filename**
	to save message 1 in the mail_folders directory

To hold messages in mail box:

& **ho** *1*	*to hold message 1 in your system mail box to read later*

To respond to a message:

& **R 4**	to *reply to message 4*

To quit `mail` with changes:

& **q**	

To leave `mail` without making any changes:

& **x**	*all the deleted messages will still be there next time*

13.4 The `biff` program

If you have a tendency to stay logged in for a long time, you might not know that mail had arrived for you for many hours. Thus, e-mail is not suited for quick conversation. If you want to know instantly when a piece of mail has arrived, then use the `biff` program:

```
% biff
```

After you have executed `biff` (perhaps in your .login file) you will be notified as soon as mail arrives, as long as you are still logged in.

13.5 Sending e-mail

The generic command to send a mail message is:

```
% mail user@machine
```

Once you have issued a command to start an outgoing mail message, the program will prompt you for the *subject*, then it waits for you to enter the text of the message. When you have finished entering text, *end* by pressing **ctrl-D**. You may then be prompted for e-mail addresses for carbon *copies*. You may abort sending with **ctrl-C**.

13.5.1 Tilde escapes

After you have entered the subject and hit return you can use several features called tilde escapes. You must type the tilde as the first character on the line if it is to be recognized as one of these special commands. The two most common tilde commands are:

~v	*once inside a mail messag, to invoke the editor*
~r	*once inside a mail message, to read-in (include) a file*

13.5.2 Aliases

A mail alias is used in place of an e-mail address to send mail to several users at once, or as a short substitute for a long address. Mail aliases live in the `.mailrc` file in your home directory:

```
alias mygroup fred@helios nancy@pluto
lynn@pluto
alias will will_russell@jri.ucsc.edu
```

You may use an editor, e.g., **vi**, to edit this file. Then

```
    % mail mygroup will
```

will initiate a message to `fred`, `nancy`, `lynn`, and `will`.

13.5.3 The **mbox** file

The file `mbox` in your home directory is where mail messages are saved if you read them but don't delete them. This file can grow extraordinarily large if you are not careful. Use **set hold** in your `.mailrc` file to eliminate this problem.

13.5.4 The forward file

Users who have computer accounts on many machines (all of which are tied to a network) have a special problem: Do you have to login to all these accounts regularly to answer mail? No. Mail can be automatically forwarded to a different account, by creating a file named `.forward` in your home directory. You must use an editor, e.g., **vi**, to create this file. The file must contain a valid e-mail address. For example, to forward your mail to your account `jack` on some other machine you might enter:

```
    jack@host.ucsc.edu
```

in your `.forward` file. If you want it to go to more than one place, separate the entries with commas. For example:

acct_name1@machine1, acct_name2@machine2

If you want to keep a copy in the account from which your mail is being forwarded, add:

```
    , \your_acct_name
```

to the previous line. **Caution**: Do not have `.forward` files point to one another.

13.6 World-wide computer networks

Mail messages which are sent over the Internet can travel to the other side of the world in a matter of seconds. To achieve some semblance of organization in such a vast domain of host names, some conventions have been developed for choosing addresses and host names.

13.6.1 Address conventions

The generic form is:

```
user@host.domain.typ
```

where the suffix typ is generally one of these three letter identifiers

```
com              Commercial
edu              Education
gov              Government
mil              Military
org              Organization
net              Network
```

For example:

```
claspac@jri.ucsc.edu.
```

International addresses include geographical information after the typ suffix.

13.6.2 USENET

Before the privatization of the Internet, most UNIX machines were connected to an informal collection of telephone-accessible machines using **uucp** (the Unix-to-Unix Call Program). This loose collection of UNIX hosts is called the USENET.[1] **The uucp** program allows two UNIX hosts to talk over modems and a telephone line sending plain ASCII text at some slow speed. Once communicating, the two hosts can forward electronic mail messages. This loose network has been in service for many years and until recently UUCP was the easiest way for small companies and individuals to connect to the world for exchanging e-mail.

E-mail addresses for **uucp** on USENET usually have the form:

```
host1!host2!...!hostn!user
```

An example is:

```
cats.ucsc.edu!jri!claspac
```

13.7 E-mail replies to messages

The reply feature in most e-mail programs is guaranteed to work if the other user is on the same machine as you are. Internet addresses of the formats we have shown usually work well also. But sometimes it is impossible for **mail** to figure out exactly where USENET mail came from, since these messages have to be forwarded over so many different computers. Therefore, the reply feature in **mail** is unreliable in these cases and you may want to rewrite the address by hand. Complex addresses are best to put in your **.mailrc** file as aliases.

---

1. You can obtain a USENET map showing the common regular telephone calls which occur between large UNIX installations. This map is in the postscript format and is available from the URL:

```
ftp://jri.ucsc.edu/images/postscript/usenet_map.ps
```

Chapter 14 Shared Data: Internetworking

The allure of the Internet is based on its facilities for sharing files. For example, this book was created in a collaborative effort aided by the Internet. The files which make up the chapters were stored on one machine but they were accessible over the network to all of the co-authors. Without the Internet we would have been exchanging floppy disks or magnetics tapes and there would have been a constant worry about which copy of a file was the latest. With the Internet we were able to keep one set of files on one machine accessible to everyone.

14.1 Transferring files between machines

File transfer methods depend on the types of machines and connections involved. Some alternatives are given in the following table.

Table 14-1. Data file transfer summary.

Type	Modem/Phone	Internet
IBM PC <-> UNIX	mskermit	ftp
	procomm	telnet
Apple II <-> UNIX	AppleWorks	

Table 14-1. Data file transfer summary.

Type	Modem/Phone	Internet
MAC <-> UNIX	kermit	telnet
	microphone	fetch
UNIX <-> UNIX	mail	mail
	uucp	rcp
	tip	ftp
		telnet
Other <-> UNIX	tip	ftp

14.1.1 kermit, a terminal emulator

The kermit program is a terminal emulator; it makes your micro-computer look like a terminal. This is one way to connect PCs or Macintosh computers to a UNIX machine. Terminal emulators typically emulate several brands of terminals.

The DOS program mskermit emulates its own brand of terminal called mskermit227 on UNIX. The Macintosh program **kermit** emulates a vt100. These terminal emulation programs can also be used to transfer files.

14.1.2 **ftp,** file transfer program

Versions of this program are available on any machine connected to the Internet. This program has versions that run on UNIX and the IBM PC. From the Macintosh, you should use **Fetch** instead.

14.1.3 **telnet,** an Internet terminal emulator

Versions of this program are typically available on any machine connected to the Internet. This program acts as a terminal emulator and as a file transfer program. From the Macintosh, **telnet** emulates a vt100.

14.1.4 **tip,** terminal interface program

This program runs under UNIX and allows you to call out from any UNIX machine, using phone lines and a modem, to any other computer accessible over the phone. This program will also allow ASCII files to be transferred between UNIX machines.

14.1.5 **rcp,** remote copy program

If George, who has an account at MIT on a machine called `cisvax`, gave me permission (that is, his password), I could give the command:

```
% rcp -r paper george@cisvax.mit.edu:
```

to copy the entire directory, `paper`, from my account to his.

14.2 Multi-file transfers using UNIX

One of the most difficult Internetworking tasks to accomplish is the transfer of a large number of files, or an entire directory hierarchy. One method, **rcp**, has been mentionned above. Here is a summary of programs that can be used to approach the task of transferring an entire hierarchy of files:

Table 14-2. *Multi-file transfer utilities.*

Program	Explanation
ftp	used to get or put *text or binary files*
tar	tape archiving or file archiving; used to convert a collection of files and directories into one large binary file and to extract them later
uuencode	used to convert any binary file into a short-line ASCII format suitable for transfer via e-mail, tip, or uucp
uudecode	used to convert uuencoded files back to their original binary form

Table 14-2. *Multi-file transfer utilities.*

Program	Explanation
rcp	used to remotely copy files and directories over the Internet
compress	used to compress a file, usual after an archive is made using `tar`. After it is compressed it may be uuencoded for transfer via mail or left as a compressed binary for transfer using ftp.

14.3 `ftp`, file transfer program

In the early days of UNIX, software was distributed on large magnetic tapes. Now, it is distributed on CD-ROMs, or over the Internet via **ftp**. The file transfer program is not only a UNIX tool, but also comes with all systems that have an Internet-TCP/IP connection. This wide availability makes **ftp** one of the handier tools for transferring files between networked PCs and UNIX.

14.3.1 Sample session

Here is a recorded script of an **ftp** session from a DOS machine to a UNIX machine:

```
C:\mydir> ftp
ftp> open 128.114.131.152
Connected to 128.114.131.152.
220 jri.ucsc.edu FTP server ready.
Name (128.114.131.152): anonymous
331 Use e-mail address for password.
Password: me@myhost.ca
230 User anonymous logged in.
ftp> type binary
ftp> cd pub
ftp> ls
image.ps       menu         README.txt
ftp> get image.ps
ftp> quit
```

14.3.2 File Types

ftp (like **kermit**) makes a distinction between binary files and text files. You should be sure that you have the file type set correctly so that text will be filtered properly. Binary files should only be sent with type *binary* or else they will be filtered inappropriately during the transfer. Images, Word files, program executables, and archives are all examples of *binary* files.

After the ftp> prompt, all of the commands which may be use are shown in Table 14-3.

Table 14-3. *ftp command list*

!	cr	macdef	proxy	send
$	delete	mdelete	sendport	status
account	debug	mdir	put	struct
append	dir	mget	pwd	sunique
ascii	disconnect	mkdir	quit	tenex
bell	form	mls	quote	trace
binary	get	mode	recv	type
bye	glob	mput	remotehelp	user
case	hash	nmap	rename	verbose
cd	help	ntrans	reset	?
cdup	lcd	open	rmdir	
close	ls	prompt	runique	

Table 14-4. *most useful ftp commands.*

FTP Command	Explanation
close	used to end the current connection
mget	to get multiple files from the remote host
mput	to put multiple files onto the remote host
type ascii	to transfer the next batch of files with a text filter that adjusts newline characters nicely
type binary	to transfer the next batch of files without any filtering whatsoever
quit	to close connection and exit program

Most of the commands shown in this table don't come up very often. Opening a connection, putting or getting a file, and quitting are usually enough.

You should cluster the files you want to send into a single directory before you start sending files. If you are receiving files, than you should also make a directory specifically intended for holding the files you will collect. While in this working directory, you can start up **ftp**. Then, once you have connected to the remote site, you will usually need only the commands shown in Table 14-4.

14.4 Anonymous `ftp`

The file transfer program is the most widely used mechanism for transferring files over the Internet. Ordinarily when you connect to another machine using `ftp`, you must specify a valid login name and password. Some generous universities and businesses operate UNIX hosts which are set up to allow public access to a small portion of their files. These machines are called *anonymous* `ftp` *servers*. As with any other service on the Internet, you find out about anonymous `ftp` servers by word of mouth, and by hunting around, and by reading books like this one. A list of some anonymous ftp servers and the kind of data they have to offer is in Table 14-5.

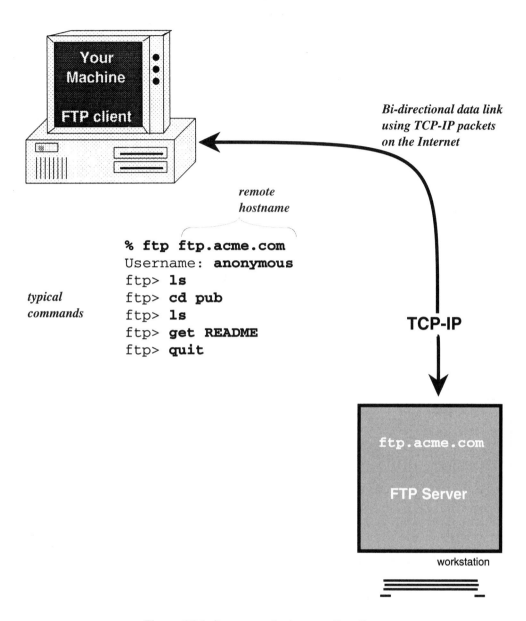

Figure 14-1. *ftp: conceptual connection diagram.*

Table 14-5. *Anonymous ftp servers*

Anonymous FTP Servers	Description
bcm.tmc.edu	DOS programs for using gopher, NFS & NetNews
boombox.micro.umn.edu	MAC and UNIX programs for using POP mail, DOS version of binhex
mail.unet.umn.edu	SLIP and other software
cs.orst.edu	X11R4 X-windows software, GNU Free Software Foundation packages for C compiler and other utilities, source code for graphics programs, UNIX version of PKZIP/PKUNZIP, and lots more
etlport.etl.go.jp	UNIX and X utilities, Mime (a UNIX mail utility)
ftp.acns.nwu.edu	UUCP for DOS, TCP/IP utilities for DOS, C++ example code
ftp.doc.ic.ac.uk	Scientific research information, maps, images, and programs with topics ranging from Astronomy, Biology, Geology, and Meteorology.
ftp.omnigroup.com	NeXTSTEP World-Wide Web software
ftp.sdsc.edu	Image manipulation software for many different platforms. Conversion utilities for almost every image format (tiff, GIF, pict, etc.)
ftp.ucsc.edu	Federal Office of Management & Budget Data, NSF net policies, Kerberos source code and related materials, Mosaic for MAC, Mosaic and otherutilities for DOS
ftp.uu.net	A huge ftp site with software for everything from Amiga to VMS

Table 14-5. *Anonymous ftp servers*

Anonymous FTP Servers	Description
otter.stanford.edu	Mathematica and Maple scripts for learning topics in higher mathematics
prep.ai.mit.edu	Source code for UNIX EMACS editor
sonata.cc.purdue.edu	NeXTSTEP UNIX resources
wuarchive.wustl.edu	Another huge ftp site with software for everything (Multimedia, programming languages, for many machines)
tsx-11.mit.edu	Linux operating system source and utilities

14.5 File archiving

Transferring file hierarchies through e-mail

When the connection between two machines will only support ASCII transmission of short lines, as with **uucp** or **mail**, then sending whole directories can be more difficult. A UNIX utility called **tar** is used to create tape or file archives which contain entire directory hierarchies. This is similar to **Stuffit** files on the Macintosh or **ZIP** files under DOS.

Here is a way to send a whole file hierarchy, sendir, in three steps.

1. Archive the hierarchy sendir into a **tar** file:

```
% tar cvf tempfile.tar sendir
```

2. Encode the archived hierarchy as ASCII for transmission:

```
% uuencode tempfile.tar < tempfile.tar >
                         send.uu
% rm tempfile.tar
```

3. Mail the ASCII encoded and archived hierarchy:

```
% mail recipient@destination
Subject: file hierarchy
~r send.uu
^D
```

Later, at the other end of cyberspace:

1. Receive the file from mail:

```
% mail
>   1 sender@source.ucsc.edu
& w 1 receive.uu
```

2. Decode the ASCII file into the binary `tar` file archive:

```
% uudecode receive.uu
% rm receive.uu
```

3. Extract the files and directories from an archive:

```
% tar xvf tempfile.tar
```

Chapter 15   The UNIX Shell

15.1 Introduction to the C-Shell

A *shell* under UNIX is the program executed by the operating system when you login. Your shell is a program (written in the programming language C) which is executed like any other UNIX command. There are two standard shells which come with UNIX, the Berkeley C-shell (**csh**) and the older and more primitive Bourne shell (**sh**).

15.1.1 Logging in

UNIX is a multiuser operating system. Every user has an entry in a file called `/etc/passwd`, which looks like this:

```
will:XoUq3x4eAg:123:423:W Russell:/b/i/will:/
          bin/csh
```

in which the field meanings are:

```
Account Name:Public Key:UID:GID:Real Name:Home
          Dir:Shell
```

When you login, UNIX checks the password information and then executes the program whose complete path is listed in the shell field of the password entry. In most cases that shell is `/bin/csh` or `/bin/sh`. The super-user may specify which program becomes your shell by modifying the `/etc/passwd` file. In BSD, any user may change their login shell by using the **chsh** utility. The next time you login, the new shell you have selected will be the program invoked instead of the **csh**. With the **csh** as your login shell, some commands are executed automatically each time you login. The first thing that the **csh** does when it is invoked is to read these

startup commands from a file in the user's home directory called
.cshrc (the **rc** stands for read on call).

15.1.2 **The .cshrc** file

Each of the commands in this file are executed just as if they had
come from the user's keyboard. After the **.cshrc** is sourced another
startup file called **.login** is also *sourced*.[1] After the startup files have
been processed, the shell prints a prompt and waits for your text
input. Each line of text you type is one command the shell will execute. The C-shell (`/bin/csh`) was designed to increase the UNIX
user's productivity. This is primarily accomplished by providing
shortcuts in issuing commands.

15.2 Filename expansion

A user may specify a pattern in place of a complete file name. This is
particularly useful in manipulating large numbers of regularly
named files, for example C files, which all end in **.c**.

15.2.1 Filename matching characters

Most programs take files as arguments on the command line, and it
soon becomes tiresome to type out the filenames in their entirety.
Special characters are used by the shell to help you abbreviate file
names with a simple shorthand. These characters are called *global
filename expansion* characters or *globbing* characters.

15.2.2 Filenaming conventions

You may increase the effectiveness of file globbing if you group similar files by using common prefixes or suffixes in the file name. For
example, all C program files end in **.c**. Therefore searching for all
occurrences of a pattern in a program is done easily with:

```
% grep "pattern" *.c
```

---

1. A file can be *sourced* automatically at login or by hand with the command %
   source myfile. In either case, the shell reads the text of the file as if
   you had typed the commands from the keyboard. In other operating systems,
   such files are called *batch files*; under UNIX they are known as *script files*.

Table 15-1. *csh globbing characters.*

Glob Character	Meaning
?	match any single character in the real file name
*	match any combination of characters in the real file name in place of the star
[0-9]	match any character 0 through 9 in place of the square bracket expression
[xyz]	match an x or y or z in place of the square bracket expression
~	match your home directory
~user	match the home directory of user

Note: These characters work *only* when used as arguments to a C-shell command. The command line is expanded by the shell before the command is executed.

Make up your own suffixes or prefixes. Grouping files with common prefixes has the added benefit that all files named with the same prefix are listed together in the alphabetical directory listings produced by **ls.**

15.2.3 Globbing examples

`text[0-7]*`	will expand to all files in the current directory which start with text followed by a digit 0 through 7 and then any other characters.
`ls *.[ch]`	will expand to all files ending with `.c` or `.h`.
`*/Makefile`	will expand to all files called `Makefile` in any directory.

The command **ls** is useful for printing the results of a file name expansion before you do something to them:

`% ls *.[ch]`	list all files with a dot **c** or **h** suffix.

The **rm** command is used to remove files:

```
% rm !$          the !$ is a short hand for the last word from
                 the previous command, in this case the last
                 word was *.[ch]
```

15.2.4 Using the dot character in filenames

Filenames may contain any characters, although some characters can cause problems (e.g., globbing characters or white-spaces). Filenames with multiple parts may be broken up, by using characters such as underscore '_', dash '-', or period '.' for example:

db_input, db-input, db.input.

It is not advisable to use a blank or tab character in UNIX filenames. Another character you should not use is the forward slash '/'. The preferred separator in multipart names is the period '.' because it has special meaning to the shell.

15.2.5 File redirection, standard input and output

The *greater-than* and *less-than* characters have special meaning to the C-shell. These characters are processed *before* the command is executed. The meanings will be clear from these two examples.

1. The UNIX utility **cat** normally prints files to the screen, which is also called the *standard output*. The redirection character **>** causes the standard output to be changed (redirected) from the screen to a file (called `all` in this example):

```
% cat file1 file2 file3 > all
```

2. The UNIX utility **expand** translates tabs in the input into blanks. It normally reads from the keyboard or *standard input*. In this case, the redirection character **<** causes the standard input to be changed (redirected) from the keyboard to the file `all`:

```
% expand -4 < all > notabs
```

which then saves its output in the new file, `notabs`. Note that both the standard input and standard output have been redirected in the same command.

15.2.6 The shell variable `noclobber`

Redirecting the output into the file `all` will overwrite its previous contents, if it already exists. You can prevent this if you set the shell variable `noclobber`:

```
% set noclobber
```

With `noclobber` set, the C-shell will warn you if you attempt to overwrite (that is, clobber) a file with output redirection. People who want this protection all of the time would put the set command shown above in their file, `.cshrc`.

15.2.7 Output redirection append

If you want the redirected output to be *appended* to the end of a file (rather than overwriting the file), then use the special output redirection symbol `>>`.

15.2.8 The semicolon

The semicolon allows you to specify multiple commands on a single line of input:

```
% cd .. ; more test_file
```

15.2.9 Connecting commands with a pipe

Like the semicolon, the pipe character `|` breaks up a single line of input into multiple commands. However, for each command, the standard input is connected to the standard output of the previous command. The first command in the pipeline has the terminal as its standard input, the last command has the terminal as its standard output. The command:

```
% grep "russell" phonelist.txt | sort > list.rus
```

uses both a pipe and output redirection. Actually, two programs are invoked with this one command. The pipe sends the output of `grep` to the input of `sort`. The output of `sort` is then placed in a file called `list.rus`. The pipe facility avoids the need to create temporary files to hold intermediate results.

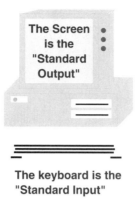

The keyboard is the "Standard Input"

Figure 15-1. *Default standard input and standard output.*

15.3 Aliases

The C-shell provides an alias mechanism. This allows you to rename a frequently used command to something more natural or easier to type:

```
% alias print `lpr -Plocal'
```

15.3.1 The mechanics of alias expansion

The C-shell looks at the first word of every command to see if an alias exists with that name. If there is a matching alias, then the text of the original command is substituted with new text from the alias definition. This is handy for reducing the amount of text you have to type for frequently used commands.

Aliases can be built on top of other aliases. The alias substitutions are invoked repeatedly until the command has no matching aliases.

The rich feature set of the C-shell makes it both an incredibly powerful tool and a frustration at times. Unfortunately, the online manual pages describing the C-shell are cryptic at best. Even so, a couple of afternoons sitting with the manual pages showing in one window and your own C-shell experiments in another window will leave you wondering how you ever got along without a history mechanism and variable references.

Table 15-2. *CSH alias examples.*

Alias Examples	Explanation
% **alias h history**	command shorthand for the history command
% **alias ll 'ls -la \!*'**	the \!* in an alias definition allows any arguments given to the user's command (ll) to be passed on to the substituted command (ls -la)
% **alias mail Mail**	typical alias used to distinguish between different mail front ends
% **alias moe more**	Frank's 'r' key sticks, so in order to make up for that...
% **alias see 'cat -v \!*'**	to examine binary files the **cat** program's **-v** option works well

Table 15-3. *Interactive commands and their prompts.*

Command	Prompt	Description
csh	%	The C-shell, the program used to invoke other programs and used for executing shell scripts. It is usually the program started when you login.
sh	$	The Bourne shell, an earlier, more primitive version of the C-shell
mail	&	The electronic mail program is used to examine, remove, reply, and save electronic mail messages.
more	--More--	The more program lets you display lines of text from a file so that they don't spill off the screen. When a page of text is displayed, the More prompt is printed and the program waits for you to hit the space bar to continue.
vi	none	The vi text editor allows you to enter command text without a prompt. Some long commands are started by a colon.
gdb	(gdb)	The GNU program debugger. A tool used by programmers to help trace errors in their C programs.

Chapter 16   Conclusion

In summary, we have seen that the Internet has been growing both rapidly and steadily, first with e-mail traffic, more recently with *anonymous* **ftp** traffic, and now with WWW traffic. As the ease of file-sharing increases, the new electronic web of human consciousness thickens, as predicted by Teilhard de Chardin in 1924.

The urgent issue now, for our further evolution, is the continued free growth of the Internet and the WWW, without the hindrance of government or commercial restrictions. Hence, it is imperative that we all take our places in the New World of multimedia file-sharing without delay. And yet, there are impediments to jacking-in right now.

First of these is the difficulty to find an Internet Access Provider. For this, we just have to ask, and keep on asking, our local Internet providers, for SLIP or PPP service. As more of us ask, the law of supply and demand will act in our favor.

Second, there is a cultural gap of knowledge: Where do we find the software, and how do we install it and get started as new immigrants to the promised land?

Third, there is the hurdle of learning the language and finding our way in this New World of the noosphere.

By discussing solutions to these three problems, we hope we can be helpful in your exploration in, and creation of, the Future of the Internet.

Appendix 1   WWW Glossary

AU   *AUdio*. Digital audio format introduced by Sun Microsystems.

ANSI   *American National Standards Institute*.

AVI   *Audio Video Interleave*. Digital audio and video format introduced by Microsoft.

baud   Officially the reciprocal of the shortest pulse width in a data stream, but usually taken to mean bits-per-second.

bit   One bit of data can be a number 0 or 1 or a voltage (on or off.)

boot   The process of turning on and starting up the software on a computer.

bootp server   *Boot Protocol Server*. The boot protocol can be used to dynamically establish a new Internet address for a client machine each time it boots. For some operating systems, the protocol also allows for diskless work- stations to be clustered around a *bootp server*.

bootstrap   To use a *simple* version of a software or hardware system as the tool for building a more complete version of that same system.

byte   A byte typically refers to 8 contiguous bits of data, which can represent a number in the range 0 to 255.

CCL   *Communications Control Language.* The language used on some computers to write dial scripts for using a modem.

DCT   *Discrete Cosine Transform.* A version of FFT.

domain   (1) A term used to describe an institution which uses a well-known set of Internet addresses. For example, our machines are in the domain `ucsc.edu` .

                 (2) A term used for one 8- to 16-bit section of an Internet address. Internet addresses are divided into a sequence of bits, with sections for the *domain*, the *subnet*, and the *host*.

FFT   *Fast Fourier Transform.* A mathematical transformation used for representing a periodic function in a compact code.

gateway   A gateway is a computer which forwards data from one segment of the Internet to another. Network providers will typically supply you with the address of a gateway machine if you need it.

GIF   *Graphics Interchange Format.* Bit mapped graphics standard introduced by CompuServe.

helper   Application program launched by a browser in response to a hypertext link to a particular type of file.

host   (1) Another word for computer. A term generally used to refer to a computer providing data to other computers on a network or dial-up line.

                 (2) The term used to describe the last 8 to 24 bits of an Internet address. See Figure 8-3 on page 83.

HTML   *Hyper Text Markup Language.* Format language for hypertext documents with inline graphics adopted as a standard by the WWW.

HTTP   *Hyper Text Transfer Protocol.* Standard for file transfer protocol adopted by the WWW.

JPEG   *Joint Picture Experts Group.* Standards organization for digital image compression. Also, the standard adopted by it, using DCT.

kludge   Pronounced *klooj*, this word comes down through the years as a colorful bit of engineering jargon. It is generally used to describe a quick-and-dirty implementation added to a poor design.

MPEG   *Motion Picture Experts Group.* Standards organization for digital audiovisual compression Also, the standard adopted by it, using DCT.

MPG   *MPeG.* See MPEG.

nameserver   A term used to describe a machine which matches host names with Internet addresses. This mapping allows most user applications to accept a human-readable host name in place of a 32 bit Internet address. Network providers will typically supply the address of one or more nameservers for their customers.

NCSA   *National Center for Supercomputer Applications.* A government subsidized laboratory at the University of Illinois, where **Mosaic** was created.

packet driver   The name of a program used to provide the lowest level interface to a network card. Each different brand of network card (also called network adaptor) has its own specific packet driver. TCP/IP applications communicate with the network by calling functions provided by the packet driver. The packet driver paradigm has since been modernized with the invention of the dynamically linked library. Under Windows it is possible to use the WINSOCK.DLL to provide a standard set of functions for accessing the network. Some versions of the WINSOCK.-DLL are written on top of the old packet driver scheme and some versions of the WINDOWS.DLL stand alone.

PATH
The name of a shell variable which is used under UNIX, DOS, and Windows to guide the search for an executable file. When you type a command, the shell looks through each directory of your PATH to find a file named *command*.

PPP
Point-to-Point Protocol. An improved package similar to SLIP which more gracefully handles establishing dynamically assigned Internet addresses.

SLIP
Serial Line Internet Protocol. A TCP/IP packet management standard for connection to the Internet using modems and serial lines.

SND
SouND. Digital audio format introduced by NeXT Computer, Inc.

subnet
A term used for one 8- to 16-bit section of an internet address. Internet addresses are divided into a sequence of bits with sections for the *domain*, the *subnet*, and the *host*.

TCP/IP
Transmission Control Protocol/Internet Protocol. The Internet Protocol specifies the format of 1s and 0s to be sent over the network in packets. TCP specifies how those packets can be used to provide reliable two way communications.

TCP stack   *Transmission Control Protocol Stack.* A suite of layered software pieces used to provide the means for user-level applications to send data through an add-on piece of hardware such an ethernet card, modem card, or other network adaptor. The layers from top to bottom are: User Application, Dynamically Loaded Library of standard networking functions, Packet Driver providing hardware-specific functions, and last, the hardware ethernet or serial card add-on.

TSR   *Terminate and Stay Resident.* A TSR program is usually one that you launch from your `autoexec.bat` or `config.sys` file. This was the mechanism used before dynamic libraries came along for sharing a common set of instructions between several applications. The shared code would be loaded by the TSR and stay in memory, where it can be accessed by other programs. The address where the shared code will live is often passed as a command line argument to the TSR program. The same address is used as a configuration parameter in the other applications that need to know where to look for the shared code.

USGS   *United States Geological Survey.* A branch of the federal government responsible for producing and updating maps and other geological information resources. They have some of the most interesting and practical data available on the Web.

VFW   *Video for Windows.*

WAIS   *Wide Area Index Server.* A program for indexing text files for the WWW.

WAV   Digital audio format introduced by Microsoft.

WIN32S   32-bit computing support software. An additional set of software you can download from Microsoft to work with 32-bit Windows applications (`ftp.microsoft.com`).

WWW   *World-Wide Web.* A network of interconnected hypertext pages built on top of the Internet. The pages are examined and traversed using a hypertext browser such as **Mosaic**.

Appendix 2 **Webography**

This appendix lists some of the many useful jump stations on the WWW[1]. First, the tops of the tallest trees.

The super sites

Some jump stations are so good you can get lost in them for days. Here are our favorite super sites.

- CERN: The European Center for Nuclear Research is the high-energy physics establishment in Geneva, Switzerland, where the WWW was created by Tim Berners-Lee in 1989. Contains many official documents as well as a major jump station.

  ```
  http://info.cern.ch
  ```

- EIT: Enterprise Integration Technologies. Here you will find an outstanding hypertext book on the WWW by Kevin Hughes, as well as a large jump station.

  ```
  http://www.eit.com
  ```

- NCSA: National Center for Supercomputer Applications, where **Mosaic**, the first HTML browser, was created by Marc Andreeasen in 1992, which led to the explosive growth of the WWW beginning in January 1993. Another massive jump station, heavy on construction details such as software specifications and where to find software.

  ```
  http://www.ncsa.uiuc.edu
  ```

---

1. These have been checked in November 1994, but may change at any time.

- GNN: Global Network Navigator. Commerce, news, jump stations, etc.

  ```
  http://nearnet.gnn.com/gnn/wel/wel-
     come.html
  ```

- WebCrawler: The super index to the WWW. Check out the Top 25.

  ```
  http://www.biotech.washington.edu/Web-
     Crawler/WebQuery.html
  ```

- LISTSERV: The super index to listservs.

  ```
  http://www.clark.net/pub/listserv/
     listserv.html
  ```

Major sites

A major site is any URL that can be found in the directories of the super sites listed above. There are hundreds of these. They are usually listed in categories such as education, commerce, and so forth.

Commercial:

- Commerce Net: An experiment in business.

  ```
  http://www.commerce.net
  ```

- One World: Sort of yellow pages.

  ```
  http://oneworld.wa.com
  ```

- Internet Shopping Net: A virtual mall.

  ```
  http://www.internet.net
  ```

- Internet Information Mall: Another virtual shopping mall.

  ```
  http://marketplace.com
  ```

- Netscape Communications Universe: A jump station.

  ```
  http://www.mcom.com
  ```

Education:

- NOVA: Nova Southeastern University. A virtual university and extensive data base.

  ```
  http://alpha.acast.nova.edu
  ```

- GNA: Globewide Network Academy. An association of virtual universities.

```
http://uu-gna.mit.edu:8001/uu-gna/
    projects/list.html
```

- RPI: Rensselear Polytechnic Institute. Good jump station for multi-media resources.

```
http://www.rpi.edu
```

- EB: The Encyclopedia Britannica.

```
http://www.eb.com/eb.html
```

- LOC: Library of Congress.

```
http://www.loc.gov
```

- LBS: London Business School.

```
http://www.lbs.lon.ac.uk
```

- UT Austin: Index of WWW courseware.

```
http://wwwhost.cc.utexas.edu/world/
    instruction/index.html
```

Music:

- IUMA: Innovative site for new music in MPEG audio format.

```
http://sunsite.unc.edu/ianc/index.html
```

- The Rolling Stones: Audio and video clips of the classic R&B band.

```
http://www.stones.com
```

- The Beastie Boys: For younger listeners.

```
http://www.nando.net/music/gm
```

News:

- Internet Multicasting Service.

```
http://town.hall.org
```

- Weather reports.

```
http://rs560.cl.msu.edu/weather
```

- Wired Magazine: Very hip Internet news.

```
http://www.wired.com
```

- HotWired Magazine: More hip Internet news available on the WWW only.

```
http://www.hotwired.com
```

Photography:

- UCI Bookstore: Ansel Adams Exhibition.

  ```
  http://bookweb.cwis.uci.edu:8042/
      SlicedExhibit.html
  ```

Religion:

- American Buddhism: DharmaNet International.

  ```
  http://sunsite.unc.edu/dharma/
      defa.html
  ```

WWW Info:

- The CyberWeb: Resources for WWW (level 4) developers.

  ```
  http://www.charm.net/~web/
  ```

- Another CyberWeb: Resources for WWW developers.

  ```
  http://nyx10.cs.du.edu:8001/
      ~arichmon/Web.html
  ```

- JHU/APL's WWW & HTML Developer's JumpStation

  ```
  http://oneworld.wa.com/htmldev/
      devpage/dev-page.html
  ```

- HTML Specs

  ```
  http://info.cern.ch/hypertext/WWW/
      MarkUp/MarkUp.html
  ```

Mathematics:

- MSRI: Mathematical Sciences Research Institute.

  ```
  http://info.msri.org/
  ```

- GANG: Geometry from the research frontier.

  ```
  http://www.gang.umass.edu/
  ```

- Geometry Center: More frontier mathematics.

  ```
  http://www.geom.umn.edu/
  apps/gallery.html
  ```

- Vatican Math Exhibit: Historical mathematics.

  ```
  http://sunsite.unc.edu/expo/
  vatican.exhibit/exhibit/d-mathematics/
      Mathematics.html
  ```

Government:

- The United States: The president's home.

      http://www.whitehouse.gov

- The United Kingdom: a directory.

      http://www.open.gov.uk

- EFF: Electronic Frontier Foundation.

      http://www.eff.org

Interesting minor sites

A minor site is one among the 4,000 or more which are not directly listed on the major WWW jump stations. Here are some we discovered, one or more jumps away from the super sites.

- VMI: Visual Math Institute. The home site of author Ralph Abraham, and his group.

      http://hypatia.ucsc.edu

- JRI: JR International. The home site for authors Frank Jas and Will Russell, and their extensive software offerings.

      http://jri.ucsc.edu

- Sailfish: Surf reports from Carlsbad, California. One of our favorites, with an eclectic jump station.

      http://sailfish.peregrine.com/surf/
          surf.html

- AT&T: Directory of 800 numbers.

      http://att.net/dir800/index.html

Appendix 3 **Bibliography**

Branwyn, Gareth. *Mosaic Quick Tour for Windows*. Chapel Hill, NC: Ventana Press, 1994.

Branwyn, Gareth. *Mosaic Quick Tour for the Macintosh*. Chapel Hill, NC: Ventana Press, 1994.

Browne, Steve. *The Internet via Mosaic and the World-Wide We*b. Emeryville, CA: Ziff-Davis, 1994.

Devereux, Paul. *EarthMind*. New York, NY: Harper & Row, 1989.

Dougherty, Dale and Richard Korman. *The Mosaic Handbook for Microsoft Windows*. Petaluma, CA: O'Reilly, 1994.

Dougherty, Dale and Richard Korman. *The Mosaic Handbook for the Macintosh*. Petaluma, CA: O'Reilly, 1994.

Dougherty, Dale; Richard Korman, and Paula Furguson. *The Mosaic Handbook for the X-Window System*. Petaluma, CA: O'Reilly, 1994.

Engst, Adam C. *Internet Starter Kit for Macintosh*. Indianapolis, IN: Hayden Books, 1993.

Estrada, Susan. *Connecting to the Interne*t. Sebastopol, CA: O'Reilly, 1993.

Heslop, Brent and David Angell. *The Instant Internet Guide*. Reading, MA: Addison-Wesley, 1994.

Quarterman, John S. and Smoot, Carl-Mitchell. *The Internet Connection: System Connectivity and Configuration*. Reading, MA: Addison-Wesley, 1994.

Russell, Peter. *The Global Brain*. Los Angeles, CA: Tarcher, 1983.

Wiggins, Richard W. *The Internet for Everyone: A Guide for Users and Providers*. New York, NY: McGraw-Hill, 1994.

Wyatt, Allen L. *Navigating the Internet*. Las Vegas, NV: Jamsa, 1994.

Wyatt, Allen L. *Success with Internet*. Las Vegas, NV: Jamsa, 1994.

Index

The WEB Empowerment Book

Since this field is fast-moving, we expect updates and changes to occur that might necessitate sending you the most current pertinent information by paper, electronic media, or both, regarding *The WEB Empowerment Book*. Therefore, in order to not miss out on receiving your important update information, please fill out this card and return it to us promptly. Thank you.

Name: _____

Title: _____

Company: _____

Address: _____

City: _____ State: ____ Zip: _____

Country: _____ Phone: _____

E-mail: _____

Areas of Interest / Technical Expertise: _____

Comments on this Publication: _____

_____

_____

_____

❏ Please check this box to indicate that we may use your comments in our promotion and advertising for this publication.

Purchased from: _____

Date of Purchase:_____

❏ Please add me to your mailing list to receive updated information on *The WEB Empowerment Book* and other TELOS publications.

❏ I have a   ☐ IBM compatible   ☐ Macintosh   ☐ UNIX   ☐ other

Designate specific model _____

THE
ELECTRONIC
LIBRARY
OF
SCIENCE

NO POSTAGE
NECESSARY
IF MAILED
IN THE
UNITED STATES

BUSINESS REPLY MAIL

FIRST CLASS MAIL PERMIT NO. 1314 SANTA CLARA, CA

POSTAGE WILL BE PAID BY ADDRESSEE

TELOS®
THE
ELECTRONIC
LIBRARY
OF
SCIENCE

3600 PRUNERIDGE AVE STE 200
SANTA CLARA CA 95051-9835